Active Experience for Active Children: Mathematics, **Third Edition,** is dedicated to my husband and my son, Valentin and Lucas Garcia. My husband has been the most supportive and encouraging partner as I've pursued my interests in early mathematics education, and I cannot wait to watch as my son develops his own excitement for exploring mathematical concepts. I'd like to thank Dr. Herbert Ginsburg, for all he has taught me and for always encouraging me to think critically about children's mathematical thinking. I also acknowledge my colleagues and friends at the National Institute for Early Education Research for their invaluable and greatly appreciated support of my research.

Judi Stevenson-Garcia

Active Experiences for Active Children

Active Experiences for Active Children

MATHEMATICS

THIRD EDITION

Carol Seefeldt

Professor Emeritus, Late of the Institute for Child Study
University of Maryland, College Park

Alice Galper

Educational Consultant

Judi Stevenson-Garcia

National Institute for Early Education Research,
Rutgers University

PEARSON

Boston   Columbus   Indianapolis   New York   San Francisco   Upper Saddle River
Amsterdam   Cape Town   Dubai   London   Madrid   Milan   Munich   Paris   Montreal   Toronto
Delhi   Mexico City   São Paulo   Sydney   Hong Kong   Seoul   Singapore   Taipei   Tokyo

Vice President and Editorial Director:
  Jeffery W. Johnston
Senior Acquisitions Editor: Julie Peters
Vice President, Director of Marketing:
  Margaret Waples
Senior Marketing Manager: Chris Barry
Senior Managing Editor: Pamela Bennett
Senior Project Manager: Mary M. Irvin
Production Manager: Laura Messerly
Senior Art Director: Jayne Conte

Cover Designer: Karen Salzbach
Cover Art: matka_Wariatka/Shutterstock.com
Photo Researcher: Lori Whitley
Full-Service Project Management:
  Sudip Sinha/Aptara®, Inc.
Composition: Aptara®, Inc.
Printer/Binder: LSC Communications
Cover Printer: LSC Communications
Text Font: Times

Every effort has been made to provide accurate and current Internet information in this book. However, the Internet and information posted on it are constantly changing, so it is inevitable that some of the Internet addresses listed in this textbook will change.

Photo Credits: Alice Galper: pp. 2, 11, 13, 14, 42, 47, 93, 100, 136, 159, 160; David Mager/Pearson Learning Photo Studio: p. 127; Judi Stevenson-Garcia: pp. 19, 23, 35, 49, 56, 65, 67, 69, 85, 108, 109, 112, 140, 146, 147, 149, 152; Katelyn Metzger/Merrill: pp. 80, 126; Laima Druskis/PH College: pp. 30, 118; Patrick White/Merrill: p. 75.

Library of Congress Cataloging-in-Publication Data

Seefeldt, Carol.
  Active experiences for active children : mathematics/Carol Seefeldt, Alice Galper, Judi
    Stevenson-Garcia.
    p. cm.
  Includes bibliographical references and index.
  ISBN-13: 978-0-13-237334-0
  ISBN-10: 0-13-237334-3
  1. Mathematics—Study and teaching (Early childhood)—Activity programs. I. Galper, Alice.
II. Stevenson-Garcia, Judi.   III. Title.
  QA135.6.S44 2012
  372.7—dc23   2011018685

13 2023

PEARSON

ISBN 10:   0-13-237334-3
ISBN 13:   978-0-13-237334-0

Preface

"What can I do tomorrow?" teachers ask. "And I don't mean just another meaningless activity. I need something that will keep children involved and lead to successful inquiry learning." Grounded in John Dewey's philosophy that all genuine education comes through experience, but that not all experiences are equally educative, *Active Experiences for Active Children: Mathematics* answers teachers' questions about what to do tomorrow and on into the school year.

Given the importance of mathematics competence in today's society, teachers will need to learn how to plan and implement meaningful thematic investigations that truly educate young children, not just keep them busy. In this book, teachers are guided in planning and implementing a curriculum that will lead to a high level of involvement on the part of children and ultimately to children's academic success.

NEW TO THIS EDITION

This revised edition has been updated to include

- The most recent research-based recommendations for math experiences in the early years.

- Research-based information on children's cognitive and skill development in all math content areas, based on the *Learning Trajectories Approach*.

- Family newsletters updated to provide families with information about the mathematics their children are learning at school and suggestions for ways in which they can continue to support that learning at home.

- Books for adults and for children in each of the subject-matter areas of mathematics, updated and expanded with suggestions for their use.

- Research-based approaches to assessment, with recommendations for specific activities and questions that will allow teachers to better understand children's mathematical thinking.

- Updated observation and assessment tear-out sheets.

Approach of This Book

All of the concepts presented in *Active Experiences for Active Children: Mathematics* have been selected because they have been identified as key by the National Research Council, the National Council of Teachers of Mathematics, the National Association for the Education of Young Children, or other experts in the field. Over the past decade, several valuable resources have been produced by mathematics educators and other concerned groups: *Mathematics Learning in Early Childhood: Paths Toward Excellence and Equity* (NRC, 2010), *Curriculum Focal Points for Prekindergarten Through Grade 8 Mathematics* (NCTM, 2006), *Principles and Standards for School Mathematics* (NCTM, 2000), and *Early Childhood Mathematics: Promoting Good Beginnings* (NAEYC & NCTM, 2000). Each of the chapters in Part Two of this book has been carefully organized around the recommendations included in these works. They are clearly spelled out in Part One with attention to modifying standards for younger children. This allows teachers to know which standards they are meeting with a particular investigation, objective, or activity. In every case, however, the principles, standards, and focal points have been addressed in environments and contexts that promote problem solving, reasoning, communication, and making connections.

Because teachers need information on children's knowledge and abilities in order to plan for future instruction, the chapters focus on ways in which teachers can assess children's developing math skills. In addition to text explaining portfolios and their contents, guides for observing and documenting children's learning have been included.

MEANINGFUL EXPERIENCES

Active Experiences for Active Children: Mathematics consists of clear, concise, usable guides for planning meaningful learning experiences in math for children in child-care settings, preschool programs, Head Start and other federally or state-funded programs, and kindergarten. Primary-grade children should be engaged in active experiential learning as well, and each experience is extended to the early primary grades (grades 1–3). The experiences in this book are meaningful because they include the following attributes:

- They are grounded in children's interests and needs in their here-and-now world.

- They have integrity in terms of content key to mathematics.

- They involve children in group work, investigations, or projects based on inquiry learning.

- They have continuity: One experience builds on another, forming a complete, coherent, integrated learning curriculum for young children as well as connecting the early childhood setting to children's homes and communities.

- They provide time and opportunity for children to think and reflect on their experiences.

- They provide the teacher with the opportunity to document and assess children's learning.

AUDIENCE

This book is designed for preservice and inservice teachers of young children. It is suitable as a core or supplemental text in community college and four-year college or university early childhood courses. Although based on theory, its practicality will also be ideal for teachers who desire the best for young children but have limited training or formal preparation. Professionals working in the field of early childhood education will find that *Active Experiences for Active Children: Mathematics* supports their growth and understanding of how to put theory into practice. When used in conjunction with the other *Active Experiences* books, it provides a complete curriculum for the early childhood classroom.

ORGANIZATION

The chapters in Part One describe the foundation for planning and implementing experiential mathematics learning. They offer preservice and inservice teachers of young children an overview of theory, research, and guidelines contributed by the leading experts in early childhood mathematics. Chapter 1 illustrates how theories of learning and teaching can be put into practice. Chapter 2, on indoor and outdoor environments, emphasizes spatial arrangement and aesthetics that support mathematics investigations and activities. In Chapter 3, the book considers the importance of building home–school connections for math learning. Finally, Chapter 4 reviews research, theory, and recent developments in mathematics education that inform methodology and teaching strategies.

The chapters in Part Two are based on content suggested by the National Council of Teachers of Mathematics and the National Association for the Education of Young Children, as well as experts in the field of early childhood mathematics. There are six chapters based on the content areas. These guides include sections for the teacher and for the children.

Each chapter in Part Two begins with a section titled "For the Teacher," which identifies concepts key to learning mathematics. Goals and objectives are presented. This section discusses concrete ideas for connecting children's home and family to the school and describes how to evaluate and assess children's mathematical learning. Each of these chapters also has a section titled "For the Children," which consists of ideas for implementing the identified goals and objectives through thematic investigations as well as integrated and continual experiences.

AUTHORS

The expertise and background of the authors is another important feature of this text. Together, the authors bring a unique perspective to the book. All three worked in Head Start, child care, and other early childhood settings and thus bring an intimate knowledge of practice to the text. As teacher educators, they know what preservice teachers want and need in a mathematics text. Because all are researchers, the latest in theory and research in the field of early childhood mathematics is represented in this edition.

ACKNOWLEDGMENTS

Carol Seefeldt died in January 2005, but she and Alice Galper would join me in thanking the many people who assisted in revising this edition in order to create a more updated and comprehensive book for teachers and children. Senior Acquisitions Editor Julie Peters suggested many of the updates and, as usual, was patient and understanding during the revision process. Project Manager Mary Irvin and Photo Coordinator Lori Whitley provided much needed assistance by paying very close attention to the many details required to produce this text.

I would like to thank the following reviewers for their valuable suggestions and comments: Jacqueline J. Batey, University of North Florida; Angela Baum, University of South Carolina; Tamara B. Calhoun, Schenectady County Community College; Mary Hanrahan, Northern Virginia Community College; Dalila Maria Brito da Cunha Lino, University of Maine at Farmington.

I would like to thank the many teachers and children who have welcomed me into their classrooms over the years, to observe them, work and play with them, and most importantly, to learn from them. Special thanks goes to the director, teachers and children at Acelero Learning Center in New Brunswick, for allowing me to visit their classrooms and photograph their examples of engaging math activities and authentic mathematics learning.

Judi Stevenson-Garcia

Brief Contents

Contents

3 Building Connections to Home and Community Through Active Experiences 30

4 Connecting Everyday Experiences with Mathematical Content 42

--- **PART TWO** ---
Guides to Active Experiences 55

5 Developing Ideas of Number and Operations 56

6 Learning the Basic Concepts of Algebra 80

7 Developing Geometric and Spatial Thinking Skills 100

8 Learning the Basic Concepts of Measurement 118

9 Data Description, Organization, Representation, and Analysis 136

10 Learning to Problem-Solve 152

Active Experiences for
Active Children

PART ONE

Theory of Active Experiences

1

Experiences and Mathematics in Early Childhood: Theory into Practice

Mathematics learning builds on the curiosity and enthusiasm of children and grows naturally from their experiences.

National Council of Teachers of Mathematics (NCTM), 2000

Active Experiences for Active Children: Mathematics guides teachers in planning and implementing meaningful mathematical learning experiences for children in child-care settings, preschools, Head Start programs, kindergarten, and the early elementary grades. This book is based on the idea that children learn best through personal and meaningful experiences.

Experiences continue. They may last a couple of hours or a day or continue over weeks, even months. Unlike isolated activities that are fleeting, experiences are filled with learning. According to Dewey's philosophy of learning and teaching (1938), experiences foster learning in the following ways:

- They hold *deep, personal meaning* for children. Experiences are grounded in children's firsthand knowledge about their world; are initiated by the children; are age appropriate; and have meaning and integrity because the content stems from concepts key to mathematics.
- Experiences involve children in *group work and interactions with teachers and other adults,* promoting the skills and attitudes children need not only to perpetuate our democratic society, but also to continually improve that society.
- Experiences are covered with *language.*
- They have *continuity of learning.* One mathematical experience builds on another—forming a complete, coherent, whole, integrated curriculum for young children. Mathematics learning is integrated with literacy, art, science, and even outdoor play. Experiences also continue into children's homes and communities, connecting the curriculum and the early childhood setting to both.
- Experiences provide time and the opportunity for children to *reflect* and think about their mathematical experiences so learning occurs. Mathematics experiences require individual children and groups to organize, document, represent, and communicate their investigations so that learning is ensured.

DEEP PERSONAL MEANING

"High-quality mathematics education for 3- to 6-year-old children . . . should . . . enhance children's natural interest in mathematics and their disposition to use it to make sense of their physical and social worlds" (National Association for the Education of Young Children [NAEYC] & NCTM, 2002). Children's everyday experiences with mathematical concepts occur from a very young age, both at home and in the world outside their homes.

Mathematical experiences enhance children's natural interest because they are meaningful to young children, engaging them in *firsthand* learning in their here-and-now world; they encourage children to *initiate* some of their own learning; they are *developmentally appropriate;* and they have *meaning and integrity* in terms of their content. As with the sciences, the arts, and other content areas, problem solving is key to the mathematics curriculum (Seefeldt, 2005). In order to become mathematical problem solvers, children must have problems to solve and topics to investigate. This is when teachers build on children's interests and make suggestions for their work. Teachers encourage children to identify a problem, create a plan to solve it, execute the plan, reach a solution, and reflect on it.

Firsthand Experiences

Guiding children's learning through mathematical content that can be experienced *firsthand* guarantees a measure of meaning. On a daily basis, children encounter challenging mathematical experiences that require meaningful use of numbers, shapes, spatial thinking, and/or measurement. This learning occurs during everyday experiences—by putting toys back where they belong (classification), building with blocks and doing puzzles (properties of geometric shapes and spatial thinking), or remembering the daily schedule and playing music (patterns and extensions).

Piaget's work fully documented that firsthand experiences allow children to think about, construct, and use mathematical knowledge (Piaget & Inhelder, 1969). When children manipulate materials and objects in their environment, they gain knowledge of the physical properties of the world in which they live (NAEYC & NCTM, 2002). As children experiment with a wide variety of objects and materials, they learn that some things are heavy, others light. Some are large or small; others are round, square, or rectangular; and still others are triangular in shape. As teachers work together with children during these explorations, they help children to build their mathematics vocabulary by providing the labels that describe the children's interactions with mathematics materials and concepts.

When children act on their environment, they think about and figure out how to do things, they observe cause-and-effect patterns, and they ask questions and come up with solutions. They learn how to balance blocks, how to count the napkins needed for a snack, how to use an egg timer to take turns at the computer. They measure food for pets, pour water from one container to another at the water table, and use different-sized molds to create shapes with clay. Throughout, they are confirming or changing their ideas about mathematical concepts. These initial, often incomplete and tentative, hypotheses and schemas about mathematics build the foundation on which all subsequent learning is based.

Initiative, Choices, and Decision Making

Young children are naturally curious about mathematical concepts they encounter at home, at school, and in the world around them. They spend a significant amount of time throughout the day exploring everyday mathematical concepts during free play (Seo & Ginsburg, 2004). What allows children to benefit from mathematical experiences is the permission to take *initiative* and make independent choices and decisions. When they are at school, children choose from a variety of centers of interest. Once they have chosen a center to work in, they make decisions about which materials from the center they will use. They may experiment and try something new, or they may decide to repeat a familiar or enjoyable action using the same materials over and over again. These experiences provide children with feelings of accomplishment, because taking initiative allows children to follow their own interests. This leads to experiences that are more likely to meet children's individual needs and developmental levels.

Children are encouraged to take initiative throughout the day, not just during center time. Real problems that arise from living together offer children opportunities for powerful mathematical learning (NCTM, 2000). Each day presents the opportunity to think about who is at school and who is not, or perhaps whether there are more boys or girls present. Meal times allow children to help teachers determine whether there are enough plates, cups, and forks at each table and observe changes in volume as they pour milk and fill up their plates with different foods. They measure ingredients for cooking projects, sing songs and read stories with repeating patterns, count the number of children in line before going outside, and explore spatial relationships as they move around playground equipment.

Children are also given opportunities to experience the consequences of their choices because failure often contributes to children's learning. Teachers do not always protect children from making mistakes or from disappointments when teachers know that the result of children's decision making may be less than positive (Dewey, 1944). For example, a teacher might allow a child to place puzzle pieces in the wrong spots or watch a child attempt to place a rectangular block on the slanted edge of a triangular block, even though it is likely to fall. Teachers then assist the child in reflecting on the problem and developing a new plan. By experiencing the consequences of their choices, children have a chance to reflect, to think about their actions, and to determine which they would change and how or why a decision was or was not effective. In this way they develop mathematical vocabulary, problem-solving skills, and the ability to think for themselves.

Dewey (1944) saw another purpose for asking children to take the initiative to make choices and decisions. He wanted teachers to use more "stuff" in schools. Dewey asked teachers to include more raw materials so children could develop concepts and the ability to think independently. He believed that raw materials such as wood, clay, and paints—without any predetermined end or goal for their use—push children toward mathematical thinking and learning.

Given blocks, paper, and paint, children must make a plan and decide what to do with the materials, how to use them, and when they have achieved their goals. They are the ones who, when failing to achieve a goal, must decide how to change their actions or plans. When they reach a goal, they are the ones who experience the joy of achievement and the satisfaction that comes from thinking and learning. Learning to take the initiative teaches children not to be dependent on others, but to develop independence of thought and action (Seefeldt, 1993).

Developmentally Appropriate

Meaningful experiences are *developmentally appropriate,* which means that they are challenging for children's ages and abilities, but not too difficult. This book presents mathematical experiences for 3- to 6-year-old children that are challenging and, at the same time, achievable. It also extends standards, curriculum focal points, and related expectations to the early primary grades. Children are encouraged to build on their previous knowledge to achieve goals and objectives just above their current capabilities, development, and maturation. For this reason, it is essential that teachers know how children develop mathematical knowledge so they can accurately identify what children know and plan experiences to move them forward in their mathematical understanding.

Research shows that the more developmentally appropriate children's early years of schooling are the greater success they will experience in the primary grades (Charlesworth, Hart, Burts, & DeWolf, 1993; Marcon, 1992, 2002). In addition, research suggests that children's math skills during the early years are the strongest predictors of future academic success (Duncan et al., 2007). This is significant, considering the paucity of mathematical experiences provided for children during the preschool years (Ginsburg, Lee, & Boyd, 2008). It is the teacher's role to ensure that mathematical experiences are accessible to children and developmentally appropriate.

Content with Meaning and Integrity

Experiences have *meaning and integrity* in terms of mathematical content. For example, what mathematical content are children learning when they are asked to color three pigs pink and four pigs brown on a worksheet? Or, to mark things on a worksheet that are big and little? Because these activities have little personal meaning for children, and because children have no choice in the activity, they may learn that mathematics is a boring, meaningless activity. Experts agree that "young children possess an informal knowledge of mathematics that is surprisingly broad, complex, and sophisticated" (Sarama & Clements, 2009, p. 6). This means that mathematical experiences must live up to the knowledge and abilities children possess.

Mathematics content that has meaning and integrity is directly relevant to children's lives and current interests, fosters curiosity and exploration, and teaches mathematical concepts that are appropriate to individual children's developmental levels. Children's mathematic learning is enhanced when teachers thoughtfully introduce math concepts, language, and methods. Good teachers have always been concerned about fostering children's concept development (Bruner, 1966). Concepts are the ingredients for thinking. They are like the strands of a spiderweb where related facts are connected and organized into an ideal. Without a solid foundation of mathematical concepts, children are limited to understanding their world by dealing with isolated facts and bits of information.

For example, without a concept of *tree,* humans would have to memorize the name of each and every tree they encountered, because they could not conceptualize or categorize trees into a singular idea or concept. With the ability to group things into categories, or to think in terms of concepts, we are freed from focusing on each isolated fact. With concepts, children have knowledge of how facts and pieces of information are related and interrelated. They understand something because they have organized the information into a concept; it has meaning to them (Seefeldt, 1997).

New Approaches to Mathematics Standards and Curriculum

Experts from nearly every subject area have identified concepts key to their disciplines. These organized concepts give direction and guidance to planning curriculum for young children. All of the concepts presented in *Active Experiences for Active Children: Mathematics* have been selected because they have been identified as key by the NCTM, the NAEYC, the National Research Council (NRC), and other experts in the field.

In the past several years, several important publications have been produced by mathematics educators and other concerned groups: *Principles and Standards for School Mathematics* (NCTM, 2000); *Early Childhood Mathematics: Promoting Good Beginnings* (NAEYC & NCTM, 2002), a joint positions statement from these two organizations; *Engaging Young Children in Mathematics: Standards for Early Childhood Mathematics Education* (Clements, DiBiase, & Sarama, Eds., 2004); and *Curriculum Focal Points for Prekindergarten Through Grade 8 Mathematics* (NCTM, 2006). Each chapter in this book presents activities based on the expertise and recommendations of the authors. The joint position statement and NRC report specifically address high-quality mathematics education for 3- to 6-year-old children.

Recently, the NCTM (2006) saw a need to focus teachers on three major mathematical concepts, skills, or understandings for each grade level. It is thought that students are being introduced to too many concepts, many of which they are cognitively and developmentally unprepared to master. This has contributed to mathematics curricula that are a "mile wide [and an] inch deep" (Clements et al., 2004). The NCTM focal points are based on the most up-to-date research regarding young children's cognitive development as it relates to learning math concepts. Curricula developed following these recommendations "would teach a few topics intensely and have students master them and move on rather than teach many topics briefly and repeatedly over several years" (de Vise, 2006).

The emphasis at each grade level is on teaching a few concepts that children have been shown to be able to master at a young age, and saving more complex and sophisticated concepts and skills for early elementary school. This does not mean that young children are not capable of understanding parts of more complex concepts; only that it makes more sense to focus on what they will be able to achieve (Clements & Sarama, 2004).

The set of three curriculum focal points and related connections are the recommended content emphases for each grade level. "An approach that focuses on a small number of significant mathematical 'targets' for each grade level offers a way of thinking about what is important in school mathematics that is different from commonly accepted notions of goals, standards, objectives, or learning expectations" (NCTM, 2006, p. 1). The curriculum focal points and their connections can be used as the foundation for mathematics learning in that grade and for connections and extended understandings in subsequent grades. The document clearly states that it is essential that these focal points be addressed in environments and contexts that promote problem solving, reasoning, communication, making connections, and designing and analyzing representations (NCTM, 2006). The focal points and connections for each grade level are discussed in detail in Part Two of this book.

INVOLVING OTHERS

Interacting with the physical environment is not the only prerequisite for learning mathematics. Children's mathematical experiences are enhanced by interactions with their peers, teachers, and other adults. Both adults and peers are sources of information for children and serve as sounding boards against which children can test the accuracy of their thinking and knowledge (Maryland State Department of Education [MSDE], 1992; NCTM, 2002). Adults provide activities and materials that encourage mathematical thinking, such as books and stories with numbers and patterns, music with actions and directions, or games that involve rules and taking turns (NCTM, 2000). They ask questions and encourage children to think out loud. Not only are peer interactions important for social-emotional development, but shared experiences contribute directly to cognitive development and problem solving (Damon & Phelps, 1989). Each child in the class has different knowledge and skills, allowing children to both learn from and teach one another, sharing and building on what they know.

Adults also introduce children to the language and conventions of math. Some mathematical learning requires social knowledge that children cannot construct for themselves. For example, without an adult telling children that the word for a certain shape is *triangle,* or the name for a numeral is *five,* children would have no way of gaining this knowledge. Children are also exposed to the conventional symbols of mathematics, such as the "plus" and "equals" signs. Teachers introduce symbols in meaningful contexts, using them to represent problems children have encountered with real materials. Because of the importance of learning concepts in meaningful contexts, all of the experiences in this book are based on problem solving and involve children at play in all areas of the classroom and outdoor area, in group work and projects, and in interactions with teachers and other adults.

Play

Children are given the time and opportunity to play freely, which includes choosing the area in which they would like to play and the children with whom they would like to play. Sociodramatic play involves using props, pretending, making and following rules, and creating unconventional uses for conventional materials. This type of play leads to symbolic thought and the development of self-regulation and executive function, all of which are required for mathematical understanding (Bodrova & Leong, 2007; Diamond, Barnett, Thomas, & Munro, 2007; Piaget & Inhelder, 1969; Vygotsky, 1986). Children use symbolic play to help them represent ideas and act out stories that are bigger than the world they live in. It allows them to rise above their ordinary selves (Paley, 2004). This type of play requires abstract thinking—to use a block as a phone, to adopt the role of mommy or baby, to go on a bear hunt, or to run a pizza shop. Children will use this ability to think abstractly and to use symbolic representation as they approach mathematical problems.

Other types of play, including board games, organized circle games, outdoor play, puzzles and other manipulatives—even putting toys and blocks back in their places—are also a part of the mathematics curriculum. Each of these types of play gives children practice in observing, sorting, ordering, comparing, counting, classifying, and predicting.

Physical play is just as critical to developing mathematical concepts and learning. Research points out that children learn *in* and *out*, *up* and *down*, and other directional concepts only by experiencing themselves climbing in and out, running up and down, or being high or low on the jungle gym (Marzolf & DeLoache, 1994; Piaget & Inhelder, 1969).

Group Work and Projects

Children enjoy working together in small groups to carry out a project based on their interests. At the Center for Young Children at the University of Maryland, a group of five children and a teacher searched the entire center to find recurring patterns. They found them everywhere and recorded their findings, which were ultimately represented in graph form. Small groups allow children to engage in experiences with other children who share their interests or are on the same developmental level. Sometimes the groups and projects occur naturally and continue for days or weeks, and sometimes teachers intentionally bring together a small group of children, knowing they share common interests or with the intention of helping them with a concept yet to be mastered.

From time to time, the entire group of children will meet together. Listening to stories that involve numbers, acting out number finger-plays, singing number songs, making decisions about their classroom, sharing news, or listening to a visitor involves the entire community of children. Even for the youngest of children, these thoughtfully planned group meetings are valuable not only for learning social and language skills, but also because they can be used intentionally to encourage mathematical thinking.

Group experiences give children practice in following a common idea, debating a point, listening to others' viewpoints, and forming their own opinions. The informal give-and-take that occurs as children play with others, work in small groups, or meet together as a large group is important for several reasons. It is through these naturally occurring interchanges that children are challenged to adjust their egocentric thought, assimilating and accommodating differing points of view. By doing so, they develop new ways of understanding the world in which they live. Then, in order for children to play and work together successfully as a group, they must consider the ideas, thinking, and wishes of others (Dyson, 1987; Piaget & Inhelder, 1969). The ability to listen when you want to speak, to wait for a friend when you are already finished, or to follow a friend's lead rather than your own requires both cognitive and emotional self-regulation.

Interactions with Teachers and Other Adults

Today, it is recognized that children do not learn in isolation and that adult interaction in children's learning and development is not only valuable, but necessary (Bredekamp &

Rosegrant, 1995). If children are to learn mathematics through experiences, then teachers and other adults must carefully structure interactions with children and each individual child that are within what Vygotsky (1986) termed the "zone of proximal development." Bredekamp and Rosegrant (1995) describe teaching with a focus on the zone of proximal development as "teaching on the edge of children's knowledge" so that children are challenged to new and higher levels of thinking and learning and are able to successfully achieve these.

Dewey's idea that children's education takes place primarily through the process of sharing experiences includes an active role for the teacher and other adults. Arguing against traditional formal education in which a teacher lectures to passive students, Dewey saw the role of the teacher in experiential learning as more demanding, calling for more intimate, complex interactions with children, rather than less guidance and involvement (Dewey, 1938). Research demonstrates the importance of teacher math talk on children's learning of concepts. By observing and recording teacher talk during the day, Klibanoff and colleagues (Klibanoff, Levine, Huttenlocher, Vasilyeva, & Hedges, 2006) found that children who were exposed to more math talk during the school year showed significant gains in mathematical knowledge.

COVERED WITH LANGUAGE

Experiences and *language* go together. Math experiences are enhanced through listening, speaking, writing, and reading. "Mathematics education is (in part) education in language and literacy" (Ginsburg et al., 2008, p. 4). Children learn the language of math from a very young age, starting as toddlers with "Up!" and "Big!" and moving toward number words and symbols. They read books that follow familiar sequences, observe parents paying for groceries with cash, and draw pictures that include various shapes or patterns. Their everyday experiences with language include mathematical concepts, and parents and teachers who recognize the presence of mathematics in the world around them include the language in their everyday talk.

Shared math experiences provide children with the opportunity to talk together, recreate situations in the dramatic play area, repeat problems and solutions, and figure out new strategies. Probably every child in our country has been to a supermarket. But when children go as a group for a specific purpose, they see the store differently. Because they share the same experience, they have a foundation for communicating with one another. From the common experience of going to a supermarket or some other place in the community or school, themes for sociodramatic play, murals, and other group projects and investigations emerge. These, in turn, give children still more to talk about and listen to.

A shared experience such as visiting a grocery store also offers many opportunities for children to read and write. They may read a story about a grocery store before the trip. They can prepare a shopping list or a list of groceries their families usually purchase. After returning from the store, children enjoy writing about their adventure. Teachers place shopping circulars and a cash register with money in the dramatic play area. Children create price tags for food. Parents donate empty food containers to stock the shelves. Together, children build their language skills as well as their math literacy.

Many math experiences begin by reading a story that catches the children's interest. The experience chapters contain a large number of excellent children's books relating to the mathematics standards and curriculum focal points. A fine children's book may serve as an inspiration and motivation for learning math concepts.

CONTINUITY OF LEARNING

Some mathematical concepts cannot be mastered until the child's cognitive development allows for it. As children develop an understanding of mathematical concepts, they go through a continuous progression of thinking and learning known as a "hypothetical learning trajectory" (Sarama & Clements, 2009). In order to teach effectively, it is important for teachers to understand mathematical development and to be aware of progression in their students' thinking and learning. Because children's cognitive growth is continuous, their early mathematical experiences must also be continuous (Barbour & Seefeldt, 1993).

Experiences continue over time. They are not 15-minute activities, nor are they units that begin on Monday and end on Friday. Experiences continue, each expanding and extending the other. Time is given, so children can continue to expand and extend their ideas and work. They know as they leave school each day that when they return tomorrow, there will be something for them to continue doing, learning, and experiencing.

Preschool teachers in Reggio Emilia, Italy, understand the need for continuity of experiences. In every classroom you will find different groups of children engaged in experiences that have caught their interest. Some of these experiences do only last a week, but some larger experiences engage the children for months, or even the entire year. Although teachers may introduce a concept, such as shadows or water, the children propel the experiences with their own curiosities. The experiences continue until the children find resolutions to all of their questions or until another experience catches their attention.

When mathematical experiences are continuous, children have the time and opportunity to see relationships between facts, to develop mathematical ideas, to generalize, to extrapolate, and to make a tentative intuitive leap into new knowledge. This leap, from merely learning a number name or fact to connecting one fact to another, is an essential step in the development of mathematical thinking (Bruner, 1966).

Continuity should extend across children's early childhood years. This means curriculum experiences, assessment, planning, and instruction should all be coordinated and continuous from one school placement to the next. Thus, *Active Experiences for Active Children: Mathematics* offers suggestions for extending and expanding experiences so they can form a complete whole as children progress from preschool to kindergarten and into the early primary grades.

Just as experiences serve to integrate the curriculum and connect children's thinking, so they can serve to unite home and school. This book demonstrates how to involve parents in children's math learning. Each chapter specifies a role for children's families so that families will be active partners with teachers in the education of their children in mathematics.

TIME TO REFLECT

Children are given time and the opportunity to *reflect* and think about their experiences. Dewey (1938) maintained that it is only as children are able to reflect on an experience that they are truly engaged in learning. Reflecting on mathematical experiences can be particularly beneficial, because solutions to problems are not always immediately clear.

Reflection can take a number of forms. Children need the time and opportunity to *pull away* and be by themselves so they can think and reflect on what they are doing. Being able to pull away for a while and think and reflect on an experience is necessary.

Young children in group care or educational settings especially need space, time, and freedom to be alone once in a while. At other times children will be asked to reflect on their experiences by *organizing* their ideas, *presenting* them to others, *applying* their knowledge, *communicating* it to others, and *evaluating* their experiences.

Organization

Children can reflect on their experiences in different ways. They might create a display to illustrate what they have learned. One kindergarten group investigated rocks. With the teacher helping them, children classified different types of rocks they found in their community; counted and graphed rocks, identifying which type of rock was most prevalent; and labeled rocks and placed them on a table. The teacher added photographs of the children finding different rocks and provided a title for the display.

Teachers can help children present their ideas through bar graphs, Venn diagrams, or other types of graphic organizers. A kindergarten class at the Center for Young Children identified several interesting topics they would like to investigate. The teacher then made a graph of their votes. By engaging in the documentation process of collection, describing, and interpreting evidence of children's emerging mathematics understanding, educators are able to provide appropriate mathematics experiences and learning environments.

An individual or a small group of children might make a presentation to the entire group. Children could tell about their experiences, perhaps showing how tall the corn grew or how many seeds actually sprouted.

Children can be asked to apply their knowledge. They might use their knowledge of numbers to plan snacks for the group, select a specific number of friends with whom to play a game, or count the days until their birthday.

Dewey believed that an experience is not complete until it has been communicated to another person. That is why children are asked to draw, paint, or write about their experiences, communicating their ideas to others.

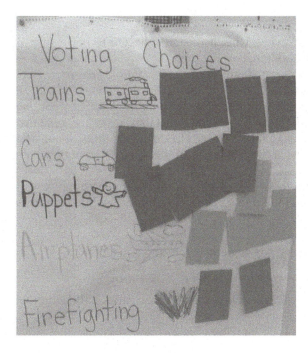

When children at the Center for Young Children voted for the topics they would like to investigate, the teacher took the opportunity to present their votes in graphic form.

Observation and Assessment

Teachers are often overwhelmed by the assessment process. Assessing children's mathematical development can be particularly intimidating if teachers are unsure of what children should know. But in order to provide developmentally appropriate experiences for children, teachers need to know what has already been learned. Formative assessment allows the teacher to assess each child's progress in relationship to the child's own development. This means that children's success is based not on how they perform in relationship to other children, but rather on how they perform in relation to what they themselves have accomplished previously. This is done through the use of observation, tasks, and informal or "flexible" interviews (Ginsburg, 2009). Regular use of formative assessment has been shown to contribute to children's learning (NRC, 2010).

"A portfolio is a purposeful collection of evidence of a child's learning, collected over time, that demonstrates a child's efforts, progress, or achievement" (McAfee, Leong, & Bodrova, 2004, p. 52). This evidence should be tied to expectations laid out by the state, the preschool program, or the curriculum. The evidence may include anecdotal records that capture what a child says and does during the course of a learning experience, pictures of children's experiences, and art or writing done by the child. For older children, entries in a math or science journal provide excellent documentation of the child's understanding of the experience.

First, teachers need to be clear as to what they need to know about what their children are learning and develop a plan for collecting specific data. Jones and Courtney (2002) suggest that there are three guiding principles in documenting early mathematics learning:

1. Collect a variety of forms of evidence. This is necessary because children vary in how they best convey their ideas.
2. Collect the forms of evidence over a period of time. A teacher who collects evidence over a period of time can see the evolution of a concept or an idea.
3. Collect evidence on the understanding of groups of children as well as individuals. Through their interactions with each other, children enlarge their mathematics vocabulary.

Further, it is necessary to frequently review what has been collected to make sure all areas of learning are assessed for all children.

Finally, children may be asked to evaluate their mathematical learning. Even 3-year-olds can be asked to think about what they did during the day. Four-year-olds, in addition to thinking about the things they did, can also begin to think about what they have learned. By 5 years of age, children can think about what they know and what they would still like to know and can make a plan to learn. They can also think about what they know now that they did not know at the beginning of the year, or when they were younger (Seefeldt & Barbour, 1998).

Teachers take time to reflect on their own work and children's learning as well. Daily they reflect on their program and the mathematics curriculum, asking themselves questions like these:

- What did I learn today about what my students know about math?

- What are individual children ready to learn next?

- What routines, interactions with the children, and experiences will I continue tomorrow?

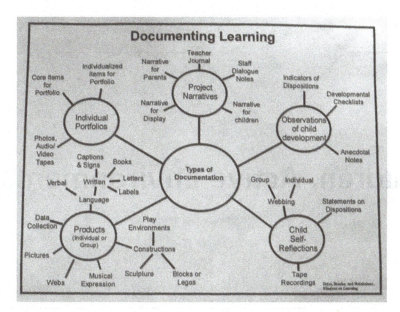

By engaging in the documentation process of collecting, describing, and interpreting evidence of young children's mathematics understanding, early childhood educators are able to provide appropriate math experiences and learning environments.

Teachers plan experiences that will allow them to assess children's learning. They observe children informally as they work and play together, talk with them individually to find out what each child understands about mathematics and what will challenge each, and collect samples of work to include in portfolios.

SUMMARY

Children learn mathematics from experiences that are meaningful, self-initiated, and engaging. Because mathematical experiences are embedded in children's everyday lives, they are of interest to children. This interest motivates children to meet the challenges of the experience and become successful math learners.

Mathematics experiences continue. When children leave school for the day, they should always know there will be something for them to continue doing when they return the next day. Teachers will also want to inform parents regarding the approach to math in the classroom. With parents on board, math learning continues at home. The fact that experiences are based on concepts key to mathematics not only gives the experiences intellectual integrity, but offers children continuity of content. And because experiences are connected to children's homes and communities, there is a continuous thread of learning in children's lives.

By using language, working with others, and having the opportunity to think and reflect on their mathematical experiences, children become independent learners who are able to regulate their thoughts and behavior, solve problems, think abstractly, and communicate clearly—all skills that are required to support their future learning of mathematics.

2

Active Children, Active Environments

Curricula have been published that apply mathematical problem solving to real-world problems; teachers are using theme centers such as the "grocery store" or the "ice cream shop" that use manipulatives and props to enhance the application of mathematical concepts.

Basile, 1999

Learning centers are ideally suited to support the development of emergent mathematics thinking in young children. As they spend time in various centers, engaging with rich materials, children explore, develop, discuss, test, and apply mathematical ideas in a variety of contexts. Centers are also ideally suited for the social interaction essential to children's construction of meaning in math as in all subject-matter areas. Rich and challenging classroom talk between children, and adult–child dialogue, foster peer-based learning. Assistance from more competent adults enables children to reach higher conceptual levels.

The range of skills that can be achieved with adult guidance and peer collaboration far exceeds what a child can learn alone or in whole-class instruction. According to Greenes (1999b), the teacher must not only model the investigative process for the children, formulating conjectures and asking questions, but also help the children to make connections among important mathematical ideas. This chapter presents general guidelines for designing environments for children—with the understanding that the learning environment acts as one of the teachers in the classroom. Attention to the organization of the classroom tells children that materials are to be respected and cared for. Areas that vary by amount of softness or space to move tell children what behavior is expected of them as they work in each center. Beyond general messages of respect and behavior, the classroom environment provides many opportunities for children to learn mathematics concepts.

If active children are to learn through active experiences, then their environment must be carefully, thoughtfully, and deliberately arranged. Spaces should be structured so children can do the following:

- Engage in meaningful firsthand learning—taking the initiative for their learning and making choices and decisions
- Work, play, and interact freely with others, both peers and adults
- Use language—talking, listening, writing, and reading—in connection with their interactions
- Experience success as they gain new skills through interaction with their physical environment
- Actively engage in exploring mathematical concepts, methods, and language through play and a range of teaching strategies
- Spend time alone or with different groups to reflect on their experiences

Beginning with the essentials—beauty, space, and aesthetics—teachers plan for children's meaningful learning experiences by deliberately arranging the indoor and outdoor learning environments. Teachers not only deliberately arrange physical environments for active learning, but also plan ways of interacting with children that foster and promote children's learning and development.

THE ESSENTIALS

Beauty

Aesthetics and beauty must be considered for young children growing up in a world that increasingly prefers highways and large housing developments to green space and historic buildings. Paying attention to aesthetics means being sensitive to beauty in the environment—in nature and art. "Such sensitivity is fostered not by talking about beauty but by experiencing it in a variety of forms" (Wilson, 1995, p. 4). It is important to note that beauty resides not only in the natural environment, but also in vibrant city neighborhoods, small historic towns, and school classrooms around the world.

In the child-care centers in Reggio Emilia, Italy, the environment is a part of the curriculum and is carefully created with aesthetics in mind. Stepping into a child-care center in Reggio, one knows immediately that the environment has been carefully arranged to simplify and order the children's world as well as surround them with beauty (Seefeldt, 1995).

Everywhere you look, there is something beautiful to wonder over and ponder. Mirrors of all types are found throughout the center. Bits of mirrors and colored glass hang in front of windows to catch a sunbeam and bounce it back to children. Long horizontal mirrors are mounted near the floor so children can watch themselves as they build with blocks or play with others.

Plants and flowers are present throughout the center in classrooms, in lunchrooms and sleeping rooms, and in the bathrooms. Children's artwork is mounted, framed, and displayed—serving not only to stimulate children to document and reflect on past experiences, but also to inform others of the experiences children are having in and out of the center. As in good practice in the United States, the home is intimately connected with the centers.

Children everywhere deserve to live and learn in environments that are aesthetically pleasing and visually appealing (Seefeldt & Barbour, 1998). Bredekamp (1993) reflects "that perhaps we, in America, have set our sights too low in our vision of excellence" (p. 13). Too often in programs for young children, little attention is given to the beauty of the classroom and outdoor space. Commercial posters and decorations take the place of objects of beauty and child-inspired art. Then, too, the connections between the world of art and the world of mathematics are ignored. As children create works of art, they learn about the use of space, line, direction, two- and three-dimensional shapes, patterns, relative measurement, symmetry, geometry, and many more basic mathematics concepts.

Space

Spaces are designed specifically to "speak" to those entering them. From a home with a beautiful entry, to a business with cubicles lined up in a row and no natural light, all spaces speak to us. Greenman (2007) says that space and objects within the space speak to our emotions and influence our behavior. A quiet corner with soft furnishings says, "Come and stay awhile. Relax." A room with high ceilings and lots of light says, "Breathe deeply. Feel free to move here." Greenman believes we underestimate the impact that the learning environment has on children's behavior and emotions. This leads to confusion between teachers and parents as to why children's behaviors are different at home and at school. Perhaps in one location, there is more organization than in the other, and the child hears different messages in the different locations about expected behavior.

Open rooms, filled with light and air, are simply and elegantly arranged. This clear, clean conceptualization of an environment is especially appropriate for active children who learn through active experiences and facilitates children's construction of beginning mathematics concepts. When conceptual learning in various subject-matter areas is integrated with artistic expression, children are encouraged to make visual or symbolic representations of their activities using a variety of media and techniques. For example, the children's re-creation of various patterns found in nature facilitates math learning.

In addition to the design and organization of the space, the way in which materials are arranged communicate mathematical concepts to children. It is possible to arrange materials in a way that supports thinking about concepts such as classification, seriation, and spatial awareness. When it is clear that objects belong in a certain place, children need to adhere to the rule to put materials away. They organize the block area by type and shape, sort play foods in the dramatic play area by type or color, and place like materials near each other—such as all materials that hold things together (e.g., stapler, paper clips, glue, and rubber bands).

Aesthetics

Preschool classrooms should be designed to communicate positive messages to the adults and children who spend so much time there each day. As Greenman (2007, p. 84) says, "Just as one would not expect to see an unhappy teacher every morning, the same logic applies to the environment." Greenman considers several aspects of the aesthetics of the classroom. The lighting and colors in the classroom contribute to the overall mood. For example, harsh florescent lighting and little natural lighting can be exhausting for long periods. Alternating lighting by adding floor lamps to the classroom or using natural lighting during the brightest parts of the day sets different moods and communicates different expectations to children.

Children's artwork should be displayed in the classroom and in the halls. Other display should include beautiful art prints, images of children and their families, or pictures children have taken in the classroom or outdoors. The display should be used to communicate to children and parents that the children's work is taken seriously and respected. Both two- and three-dimensional pieces of artwork should be displayed.

Other aspects of aesthetics include textures, sounds, and smells. These should not be ignored. Providing interesting textures for children throughout the classroom stimulates their senses and contributes to their development of classification skills and spatial thinking. Sounds and smells are often the first things we sense when entering a room, so it is important to consider the noise level in the classroom, what can be added to the room to mute echoes, and how much fresh air is allowed to circulate through the classroom. Using the environment to create a sense of belonging and comfort communicates to children that the classroom is a space designed especially for them, respecting their unique abilities and circumstances and encouraging them to engage and learn together.

INDOOR SPACES

Integrating Spaces

Organizing indoor spaces with well-equipped learning centers permits active children to engage in active experiences. Learning centers are those areas of the room that are clearly defined with either actual dividers or suggested boundaries. They contain materials and equipment organized to promote specific types of learning. The materials are carefully arranged so children can see the choices available and make decisions about which materials they will use and how they will use them (Bronson, 1995). Classrooms are ideally organized around multiple theme centers—for block construction, water exploration, art, reading, computers, gardens, a store, and an area for dramatic and symbolic play. Children are allowed to move freely among the centers, engaged with materials and other children (Greenes, 1999a).

Yet, even though areas are defined, teachers will want to work toward an integrated curriculum framework—so that mathematics concepts, for example, are integrated into social studies, arts and crafts, music and movement, literacy and language arts. Math and science form a natural alliance, and many curriculum materials are designed to integrate the two. For excellent suggestions on play materials for the classroom, see *The Right Stuff for Children Birth to 8: Selecting Play Materials to Support Development* (Bronson, 1995).

Using children's literature is another way to integrate mathematics throughout the early childhood curriculum. An important part of an effective math curriculum is a classroom library with a wide variety of math-related children's literature, both fiction and nonfiction. Books should also be placed around the classroom in areas where they will enhance the child's discovery or ability to problem-solve. For example, the chapters in Part Two of this book have extensive children's literature suggestions for teaching each mathematics concept area identified by the National Council of Teachers of Mathematics for prekindergarten through the early primary years.

Sarama and Clements (2006) suggest that long periods of time for play and enriched environments and materials (including manipulatives such as blocks and Legos that invite mathematical thinking) are critical for guiding children's exploration of mathematical ideas. The joint position statement of NAEYC and NCTM points out that "play does not guarantee mathematic development, but it offers rich possibilities" (2002, p. 11). Teachers play a major role in that they identify opportunities for scaffolding children's play—such as when block creations keep falling down or when children need help clarifying their ideas.

Math or Manipulative Areas

Although opportunities for learning emergent mathematics concepts abound in all classroom centers, children are continually drawn to an area of the room that offers a variety of play materials that may be manipulated and explored to foster math learning.

There should be enough materials available for the children that popular materials are not in short supply but also not so many materials that children become distracted or unfocused. New interesting or more challenging materials are introduced during the course of the year as children master or become tired of the old ones. Following are some possibilities for play materials that foster math concepts:

- Cardboard, wood, and plastic puzzles—varying the number of pieces and the complexity with the age of the child and including shape and number puzzles and larger floor puzzles for children to complete together

- Beads and string to foster pattern making and the copying of sequential patterns, such as materials to make pattern bracelets

- Other pattern-making materials, such as small blocks and tiles, mosaic blocks, inch cubes, links, counting bears, pegboards, and attribute blocks

- Materials for matching, sorting, ordering, and comparing (by shape, size, texture, number, color, or concept), such as baskets of shells, different-sized buttons, keys, or coins

- Games that require counting, number recognition, patterns, and matching or sorting (e.g., dominoes, playing cards, memory)

- Balance scales and various objects to weigh

- Materials for children to put together and pull apart, stack, and manipulate to observe from different orientations

- Geoboards and rubber bands

- Trays divided into sections, cupcake baking pans, or different-colored bowls to encourage sorting

- Clipboards, paper, erasable boards, and markers to record findings

Children particularly respond to games based on children's books. Cutler, Gilkerson, Parrott, and Browne (2003) suggest that teachers create games based on children's literature. Many children's books (such as those suggested in the following chapters) have built-in math content. At the Center for Young Children, children create their own games to be used by the class. The process is a wonderful exercise in problem solving.

Young children should be introduced to money even though they are not yet ready to use it correctly. For example, many children still think that the larger the coin, the more it is worth. Young primary-aged children can begin to sort coins and tell "how many" of one denomination it takes to make another.

Construction sets, Tinkertoys, Erector sets, and large Legos may find a home either with the math manipulatives or with the blocks, depending on the intent of the children's activity. There are a variety of math manipulatives on the market today—pattern blocks, number towers, various types of counters, and Cuisenaire rods, to mention a few. When considering materials to make available to children, think about the potential math concepts that might be explored using those materials. Of course, it does not take a classroom full of shiny new toys to help children think mathematically. According to Seo (2003), any object can be used as a math manipulative if children can explore mathematical ideas while interacting with the object.

The teacher will want to provide materials that excite a child's natural interest, provide many different types of problems and solutions, and promote active inquiry. Whatever active experiences spring from the children's interests or the teacher's plans,

Alice Galper

Some manipulatives help children think about multiple math concepts, such as matching, counting, and attributes of shapes.

it is important that enough time is available for children to reflect on what they learn and, if they wish, to maintain their work in progress. There should also be materials available for teachers and children to record, represent, and communicate what they have learned through webs, graphs, and various diagrams. As children play in this learning center, teachers observe their interactions with the materials, making comments and asking intentional questions so that the children begin to hear mathematics vocabulary in context. Building the foundation for mathematics understanding takes intentional planning and organizing of materials on a daily basis and throughout the school year.

Science Areas

As mentioned previously, math and science are natural allies. As children explore science concepts, they are often required to consider math concepts. The science center should provide opportunities for children to observe, classify, compare, measure, communicate, experiment, make predictions, and reach conclusions.

One teacher arranged a pitcher of water and some small cups on a table next to small containers of instant coffee, tea leaves, dirt, sand, beans, sugar, and salt. She posed a question for the children: "Which things will dissolve in water and which ones will not?" A clipboard with a checklist for children to make predictions and record their findings was placed beside the center. Children were encouraged to discuss and negotiate their conclusions. While children were engaged in the scientific process, they were also keeping track of how many items dissolved, how many children guessed correctly, which items dissolved more quickly, and whether the water level changed in some of the cups as they added more sand or beans. The primary purpose of the activity is to encourage children's scientific thinking, but many math concepts are available for children to explore as well.

Other science learning centers could be equipped with scales of all types, measurement tools, and things to weigh, measure, and balance. The teacher would pose questions such as "Which one is heavier?" or "Which is longer?" Children can record their conclusions in journals or on checksheets created by the teacher.

Screwdrivers and wrenches, along with machines to take apart—clocks, pencil sharpeners, instrument-panel boards (all of which have been safety-proofed)—fascinate children, who are curious about how things work. One group of 5-year-olds worked for days taking apart an alarm clock and recorded each step in detailed drawings that the teacher displayed to document the process and then stored for later reflection. Again, the mathematical concepts explored here might include classification of parts, such as sorting different colored wires, counting screws or bolts, arranging pieces from smallest to largest, or figuring out which piece needs to come off next—which requires spatial thinking.

Chrisman (2005) suggests a "nuts-and-bolts" science center where children develop skills in comparing, developing fine motor control, and classifying by size and shape. After the experience, children build graphic organizers to summarize what they have discovered. Examples include webs, graphs, and lists of new vocabulary words.

Art Centers

Through the visual arts, children are able to give expression to their ideas, imaginations, feelings, and emotions. This expression is necessary if children are to reflect on their experiences. Artistic representation also requires a great deal of spatial thinking, understanding of geometry, counting, and classifying. Each day, children should have a choice of whether to draw, paint, model, cut and paste, or construct something. Materials are arranged on tables or shelves that are easily accessible to children. Easels, a variety of brushes, and fresh, thick paints in a variety of colors and shades are available every day. At other times, areas of the floor, or a table or two, can also be used for painting. All types of drawing materials—crayons, markers, chalk, pastels, and pencils—are stored in open shelves for children's selection (Dighe, Calomiris, & Van Zutphen, 1998). Containers with many types of collage materials, such as tissue paper, scraps of paper or fabric, small buttons, cotton balls, or natural materials such as acorns, leaves, and twigs, are available. There are materials to construct three-dimensional art, such as empty tissue or cereal boxes, paper towel rolls, empty milk cartons, and large Popsicle sticks. There is a separate area for clay and modeling materials.

Because the visual arts give children a way to organize, reflect on, and present their ideas or emotions, art materials are chosen that enable children to do so. For example, a group of children went to the Folk Museum to see an exhibit on quilts. When they returned, they found the art center equipped with a variety of papers and cloth in various shapes, scissors, and glue—and they were given the opportunity to make their own or a shared quilt from the shapes.

Manipulating modeling clay and observing its properties, painting with tempera paints and observing drips and how colors mix, and organizing and sorting materials for a collage help children to understand math concepts and integrate them with other subject matter areas. Seefeldt and Galper (2007) emphasize the importance of displaying children's work, both to document their work for themselves and for visitors and to enhance the beauty of the classroom. At the Center for Young Children at the University of Maryland, children's paintings are framed with wood, and leaf collages are laminated for extended display.

Woodworking Centers

Woodworking involves such a variety of skills, tools, and materials that there are endless opportunities for using mathematics processes, such as classification, comparison, understanding spatial relationships, measurement, and the visualization of things in three-dimensional form. Through trial and error and careful use of questions by the teacher, children will also draw conclusions such as "That nail is larger" or "The small nail will work better." Children are endlessly fascinated by woodworking, but teachers must closely supervise and co-construct learnings with their students. Mathematical problem solving takes place as children design a plan or patterns, select pieces of wood, and measure and join the wood to implement their plan.

A place for children to construct three-dimensional objects should also be included. Children can work with any material. In Reggio Emilia, found objects—boxes, feathers, shells, sequins, paper, and silk and brocade scraps—are stored (and classified) on open shelves in aesthetically pleasing ways, inviting children to choose what materials they will use and how they will arrange them. The design and creation of three-dimensional objects helps children to master math concepts.

Book and Library Centers

The library center is a cozy and inviting area where children are encouraged to linger and daydream and share stories with each other. This area should be located in a quieter place in the classroom, away from more active centers. There should be comfortable places for children to sit, with a soft carpet and soft chairs or pillows. The books are on display for the children—with covers showing to invite their interest—as well as baskets with additional books, puppets, and flannel story pieces for retelling stories. Books should cover many genres, including poetry, fiction, folktales, picture books, informational books and materials, biography, and books composed of photographs. All children should find themselves reflected in these books; books dictated or written by the children are favorites. In addition, the stories should be about the lives of children with special needs and the families and traditions of children of diverse cultural, language, racial, and ethnic backgrounds (Blaska & Lynch, 1998). Among these books may be those that explicitly teach math, such as counting books or books about shape and space. Other storybooks often include mathematical concepts to be explored. The chapters in Part Two of this book highlight children's books appropriate for learning in each concept area.

Books will also be displayed around the room in the different learning areas: in the block building area, books about architecture and construction; in the dramatic play area, books about families, cooking, or topics the children are interested in. In one Head Start center, children went for a tour of the local food store. When they returned to their classroom, they found several books on how to set up a store, going to the store with parents, specialty stores, and large supermarkets. Children began consulting these as they created a small market with boxes, scales, and models of fruit and vegetables, all classified into sections of the center. They also became concerned with money and how to determine the cost of each product.

Although books of both nonfiction and fiction can be used to support the development of math concepts, it is important that the information be accurate. The books should further spur children to investigate something or engage in hands-on math experiences.

Sociodramatic Play Areas

The primary sociodramatic play area can be a housekeeping center, where children engage in playing out family roles they observe in their homes. Other organizational schemes are also possible, as reflected in the Boston University/Chelsea Project for Mathematics Learning, where a kitchen and a store were permanent centers.

Props reflecting children's home life are found in the housekeeping area. Some may reflect their parents' work world—briefcases, hard hats, work boots, or tools representative of parents' work. There should be props that reflect the children's lives at home, such as dishes, pots and pans, baby dolls representing all ethnic groups, cribs, baby bottles, full-length and hand mirrors, alarm clocks, discarded cell phones, calculators, computers, and clothes of all types. Other items include boxes or containers of food that their families eat, traditional and modern clothing representing the families' history and culture, and books with recipes children are familiar with.

Based on children's experiences with their world, other dramatic play areas will be pertinent. Notice how teachers can build emergent math concepts into each. For instance, if children have visited a post office, then they might be interested in creating a post office with envelopes, stamps, machines to weigh objects, and cubbyholes in which to sort mail. If the class has been to a supermarket, then they may want to make their own store—complete with a cash register, money, all types of food containers, cans, boxes, bags to pack items, old cash register receipts, and other materials—so they can reenact their visit to the supermarket, taking turns being shoppers, clerks, bakers, or shelf stockers. Each of these roles involves the use of math. As "store" play continues, the play will be expanded to include more and more math concepts.

Block Areas

Blocks and spaces in which to build are essential to a math curriculum. The block building area should be large enough so that several children have space to build substantial structures and should be in an area of the classroom that is defined and enclosed enough that children will not walk through it (Harms, Clifford, & Cryer, 2005). When children build with blocks, they indulge in activities that begin to fulfill the standards for instructional programs proposed by the NCTM (2000). Block building encourages children to explore concepts such as geometry and spatial thinking, measurement (weight and

Judi Stevenson-Garcia

Teachers add materials to the sociodramatic play area that encourage mathematical thinking.

height), balance, symmetry, patterns, and data analysis. Bronson (1995) suggests the following building blocks be available for children:

- Wooden unit blocks (80 to 100 pieces per child playing), including specialized forms (arches, curves)

- Large hollow blocks

- Plastic bricks

- For children age 4 and older, various types of interlocking blocks, except metal or those smaller than one-half inch

- Outdoor building materials

Multicolored foam blocks are ideal for both building and classification and stick together differently than unit blocks, allowing children to organize them in new ways (e.g., because of the foam texture, a block may stay on top of the slanted face of a right-triangle block, where a unit block would slip off). Block areas should also provide children with opportunities to dramatize their structures by including animals and people, traffic signs and train tracks, and different types of vehicles. These additional materials encourage children to think mathematically. For example, children consider geometric properties of street signs, create parking spaces big enough for different-sized vehicles, use symmetry and measurement to make sure the sides of a home are equal so the roof is flat and even, and build pens to enclose animals and dinosaurs in pretend zoos.

Ideally, indoor blocks should be stored on open shelves with a place for each type of block. Storing all rectangular blocks on the same shelf, for example, fosters children's ability to classify. A complete set of wooden unit blocks is the best investment a center or program can make. If these are unaffordable, blocks can be made out of paper cartons. Math concepts are fostered as children observe, build, measure, compare, estimate or predict, begin to learn about spatial relations, and construct building plans.

Water and Sand Areas

Children need areas where they can explore the properties of both water and sand. Water is easy to provide. All that is needed is a low table, a small plastic tub, some plastic containers (cups, spoons, funnels, plastic tubing, straws, and basters), and enough water for children to use. Preschool children learn about volume as they pour water from one container to another. They also experiment with filling larger containers with the contents of smaller ones and make estimates about how much it will take to fill a given container.

Sand—in a sand table, a plastic tub, or an old wading pool—can readily be available indoors. As with water play, children learn beginning math concepts through the use of a variety of containers from which to pour and measure sand, or mold and shape sand into various forms. Water should be handy if children are to build with sand. Young children often enjoy exploring cause and effect, observing what happens to sand when water is added. They watch a small amount of water "disappear" into the sand and hold it together, then notice that as more water is added, it pools in the sand. Small objects can also be added to the sand table to expand children's concept of space and location.

Music Areas

The music area should be a space in which to listen to, as well as make, music. Here, children listen to a tape, operate a CD player by themselves, or play whatever musical instruments the center provides. They use props to express their movements and create dances for others to follow. Many favorite songs involve math concepts, such as the counting songs of childhood. Kim (1999) suggests that many musical experiences are closely related to mathematical knowledge. For example, "slow and fast" is a concept that young children can easily understand and that the teacher can relate to classification and comparison. Also, young children can explore a variety of patterns through musical activities, such as introducing strong and weak beats and long and short sounds. Similarly, verbal counting can be improved through vocalizing rhymes and songs. The musical instruments should be sorted according to type or the sounds they produce so that children can classify them when cleaning up.

Computer Stations

If computers are available in the classroom, they should be there as an option for children who are interested. Teachers should be engaged with the children as they work on the computer, and the time spent should be limited to less than a half hour per session. Computers can be set up with age-appropriate programs that do the following:

- Help children develop higher-order thought skills such as judging, evaluating, analyzing, and synthesizing information (Wright & Shade, 1994)
- Encourage children to engage actively to be creative, think critically, find solutions, and solve problems
- Provide for more than one child to work with a program
- Teach a concept or concepts that children are unable to obtain through an active experience or inquiry

Sarama and Clements (2009) believe that computer programs and other technology can be useful in teaching mathematics. Used well, computers offer many advantages, such as individualizing instruction, providing immediate feedback, and offering games that motivate substantial mathematical thinking.

Quiet Spaces

Children need space to be alone or to interact with one or two others. Young children may become overwhelmed by the level of activity present in the classroom and need a few moments to take a break and recharge. It may be a corner of the room with a few pillows on the floor, a small nook in the library area with a listening center, or a chair and table set up with a game or activity for one or two children. Every classroom needs a space—wherever it is, or whatever it consists of—where children can be away from the group, relax, calm themselves, and think.

OUTDOOR SPACES

Teachers may be able to consider their available outdoor space as an extension of the stimulating, well-arranged indoor learning environment. The added richness of natural surroundings and open spaces enhances possibilities for active math learning experiences. Teachers will want to expand water and sand play outdoors. Digging in the dirt and extracting different sizes of pebbles and rocks provides information to a child about the nature of the surfaces of the earth and the concepts of heavy and light, rough and smooth, and large and small. Teachers reinforce this learning when they use questions to focus children on their inquiries. For example, when examining rocks, focusing questions might be "Which ones would you put in the pile of smooth ones?" or "This one isn't big or small, so which pile should we put it in?"

Math activities occur in special outdoor spaces arranged for the young child's emergent concept development. They are also intimately connected and integrated with all areas of the early childhood curriculum, as discussed next.

Math/Science and Nature Discovery Areas

Spaces should be designated for exploration and discovery. These include the following:

- An area set aside for bird feeders, birdhouses, and birdbaths. Children can observe and record from a distance the comings and goings of a variety of birds, their nests, and the foods they eat. This provides an excellent opportunity for data collection and analysis.

- An outside sandbox. Although an indoor sand table provides children with active experiences with math, an outside sandbox has many advantages. Children can climb into it, sit in the sand while playing in it, and create on a large scale. The sand area should be adjacent to a water source. To expand the possibilities for math concept learning, props should be added, including containers of all sizes, cooking utensils, measurement tools, and sand molds.

- A carefully supervised wading pool or water table. Water play gives children essential skills in pouring, measuring, and comparing volume. Outside, much more splashing and spilling is acceptable, and water can be carried around the play yard. Many items may be added, as required by the type of investigation children are pursuing. For example, young children can explore the capacity of various containers by direct comparisons or by counting the number of cups required to fill each one.

- A garden area for various types of plants, flowers, and vegetables. This space should be carefully placed beyond the limits of children's active play and close to a water source so that very young children can be involved in nurturing the plantings. Some teachers may want to reserve part of the gardening area for impromptu digging, where children learn about the composition of soil, the insects and worms that make their homes there, and the organic matter that decomposes to produce soil. The area should be arranged to receive at least six hours of sunlight a day. In locations where this is not possible, teachers and children together should plan gardens that flourish in the shade. The garden area provides a wealth of mathematics experiences: counting, finding patterns, measuring the growth of plants, comparing the growth of two or more plants, and deciding how much water flowers and vegetables need.

These suggestions are for a planned approach to using the school yard as a math (and science) discovery center. They may be supplemented by carefully chosen trips.

Art Spaces

Just about any art activity can take place outside. From painting with water on school walls or sheds to painting with color on large brown paper strips hanging on a playground fence, children and teachers can enjoy aesthetic experiences with the knowledge that cleanup will be simple. When they explore shapes and patterns that can be drawn or constructed on a larger scale outdoors, children build math concepts. Children can draw on the hard surfaces with large pieces of chalk of various colors dipped in water. Teachers can encourage them to try patterns by repeating the colors in a predictable, rule-governed order. Their creations will wash away with the next rain. Or, they can use crayons or markers on large papers spread on a hard surface or on tables.

Modeling with clay and other materials is fun to do outside, as is building with large boxes, found objects, and other materials. Through their constructions, children learn about the attributes of things and discover which are effective and ineffective in creating satisfactory structures. Measurement and number, as well as spatial thinking, are involved in creating structures that work—and when things fall apart, children can make inferences about suitable and unsuitable choices.

Physical Spaces

Space and a variety of stationary and movable equipment foster running, jumping, and climbing outdoors. Outdoor equipment that promotes social interactions, use of language, and cooperative play, and that is rich with potential for children to form concepts of the physical properties of their world and spatial thinking, includes the following:

- Large wooden crates and boxes, boards with cleats, and large hollow blocks

- Climbing equipment that comes in several movable sections—such as a trestle unit, a climbing gate, or an A-frame unit—that can be arranged and rearranged to meet children's changing interests or needs

- Cable tables of assorted sizes, tree trunks with sharp branches removed, and sturdy wooden barrels

- Balance beams, an old log, several logs placed end-to-end, a board placed on its side, or stepping stones, patio stones, or old tires placed in a series to give children a sense of different ways to handle their bodies in space

- A wide assortment of balls of all sizes and weights
- Things to push, pull, and ride

Other Spaces

Ideally, outdoor environments should include sections with different surfaces such as grass, concrete, earth, and sand. Pine bark, cedar chips, or pine needles can be used to create soft areas, whereas other surfaces can be paved for playing organized games, which give children a sense of using their bodies in space. Play yards should have a balance of sun and shade, active areas for large motor activities, and quiet areas where a child might take a book, listen to music, or play with small manipulatives. Attention should be given to different terrains. A balance of levels can make the play yard visually interesting and provide hills for climbing and rolling down as well as flat surfaces. Outdoor pathways may be created to wind around the outside play environment to define various interest areas. They can be created of cedar chips, stones, or cement.

When discussing math concept formation, NCTM (2000) highlights the importance of tools. Teachers will want to add tools of all types such as thermometers, rulers, tape measures, scales, and containers of all sizes and shapes to aid children in their observations and explorations. Simple cameras provide an excellent way for young children to document discoveries in the outdoor environment and then later view pictures so they can see their environment from many different perspectives.

Planning for Inclusion

The physical environment can be arranged in ways that enable all children to participate to the fullest extent possible in all experiences. According to Flynn and Kieff (2002), adaptations may be applicable to inside environments, but such accommodations are *critical* for the outside.

Children with special needs (as well as those without) may profit from a multisensory approach to the teaching of mathematics.

Reducing the amount of visual stimulation in a given area aids children who are visually impaired. Teachers have found that they can add textures or raised patterns to the walls to enable visually impaired children to locate themselves in space. On the playground, children should be oriented to the major playground features that can be used as points of reference. Tactile experiences are also valuable for nonimpaired peers because they foster learning through touch. Small shelving units, with a few materials on each shelf, are helpful for children who become overstimulated easily.

Hearing-impaired children require more visual stimulation and less auditory distraction. Felt pads on tabletops, carpeted shelves and work surfaces, and the clear display of all materials and equipment will assist these children (Seefeldt & Barbour, 1998). Flynn and Kieff (2002) suggest outdoor toys and materials that use the other senses, including touch, smell, and vision. Teachers may actively foster children's understanding and appreciation of the senses and sensory impairments through active experiences with the five senses. For a chapter on the senses of the human body, see *Active Experiences for Active Children: Science* (Seefeldt & Galper, 2007).

Mallory (1998) suggests that small groups of two to four learners provide an optimal structure for fostering cognitive development and social participation in inclusive classrooms: "Given the heterogeneity that exists in inclusive classrooms, it is logical to assume that whole group activity is not likely to be an effective means for assuring that the particular needs of individual learners will be met" (p. 228). For a good discussion of specific outdoor adaptations to meet the individual needs of children with blindness or low vision, deafness or hearing loss, physical challenges, autism spectrum disorder, and cognitive delays, see Flynn and Kieff's 2002 article, "Including Everyone in Outdoor Play," in *Young Children*.

THE TEACHER'S ROLE

> Throughout the day and across various contexts—whole group, small group, centers, play, and routines—teachers need to be active and draw on a repertoire of effective teaching strategies. This skill in adapting teaching to the content, type of learning experience, and individual child with a clear learning target as a goal is called *intentional teaching.* (NRC, 2010)

Without a concerned, interested, and knowledgeable adult, even the best-equipped and best-planned spaces fall short of offering children meaningful experiences. Sarama and Clements (2006) suggest an *organized* curriculum for kindergartners. This does not mean formal mathematics pushed down from the higher grades. Effective programs are planned and systematic, and mathematics is built into all areas of the curriculum. Based on knowledge of children and of their experiences at home and in the community, it is the adult who must perform the following tasks:

- Selecting, arranging, and changing indoor and outdoor centers, making sure the spaces remain safe, inviting, and accessible to all children

- Scheduling large blocks of time during the morning and afternoon for active experiences that focus on specific mathematics concepts

- Providing a background of meaningful experiences with people, places, and things so children will have ideas to express through play

Most of all, however, it is the teacher who interacts with children in ways that clarify, extend, and expand their knowledge and skills:

- Teachers observe and supervise children as they play. Observations can focus on the total group of children or on individuals. (See the tear-out assessment instruments at the end of chapters in Part Two of this book.) The progress children are making, the skills they are gaining, and the things they still need to learn can be noted. When observation does not provide enough information, teachers present tasks or activities that require children to demonstrate specific skills. Teachers follow children's responses with questions to clarify children's thinking.

- Teachers enter into joint activities with children, working collaboratively with them on a problem or task, such as comparing seeds from four different familiar plants.

- Teachers use the language of mathematics to promote children's learning, naming things in the children's environment and giving information when needed. They deliberately use math vocabulary and emphasize the words. For example, a teacher can encourage a child to start lunch with just *half* a sandwich and ask if she'd like a *rectangle* or *triangle.* Discourse builds students' conceptual knowledge and gives teachers valuable information for assessing progress and planning next steps.

- Teachers ask a variety of questions that help children to expand concepts and to build vocabulary: "Let's count how many children are wearing red today—how many did you count?" "Is this basket light or heavy?" "Can you find something in the room that is about as long as your foot?"

- Teachers offer assistance to help a child solve a problem or achieve the next level of functioning: "Here, I'll hold the tape measure for you on this side while you pull the tape to the other end of the table, and we'll find out how long the table is."

- Teachers plan and help children select activities that are both engaging and appropriate for individual children's development and background of experiences. "If instructional materials are not consistent with the expectations of families and community members or do not seem reasonable to them, serious difficulties can arise" (NCTM, 2000, p. 369). The selection and implementation of curricular materials must be a collaborative process.

- Teachers serve as models, displaying the attitudes and skills they want for the children. They demonstrate how to do something, supporting children as they try.

- Teachers set expectations for classroom behaviors that are consistent with children's emerging cognitive and social capabilities (Berk & Winsler, 1995).

- Teachers enter into conversations with children about their work, focusing on their ideas and strategies. Lillian Katz (1993) observed that teachers often seem reluctant to engage children in meaningful conversations and focus more on giving positive feedback than talking about content, relationships, or even what the child is doing.

- Teachers carefully structure their interactions with children to move them forward in concept development through understanding of what Vygotsky (1978) terms the *zone of proximal development.*

- Teachers ensure that all children are able to take part in all facets of the curriculum. In mathematics particularly, equity must be achieved. Teachers must build on children's varying experiences—including their family, linguistic, and cultural backgrounds; their individual approaches to learning; and their formal and informal knowledge (NAEYC & NCTM, 2002).

- Teachers assess children's attitudes, skills, and knowledge in the area of mathematics using multiple methods. Through observations of children's work and focused discussions with children, teachers plan for indoor and outdoor experiences at the next level of thinking.

SUMMARY

Active children need indoor spaces that are specifically designed to foster active experiences with mathematics. Planning indoor environments begins with making certain the spaces are beautiful, designed specifically for children, and aesthetically pleasing, as well as accessible to children with special needs. Indoor spaces are arranged thoughtfully with different learning centers that engage children's interests, but math materials and concepts are integrated throughout. Centers organize the children's environment, let them see the choices available to them, and give them the means to work and play cooperatively with others.

As Dewey (1938) suggested, the role of the teacher is more complex and more intimate when children are actively engaged in experiential learning. Teachers schedule large blocks of time for children's indoor experiences. They actively teach, guide, observe, focus, and interact with children. No environment is a learning environment without a teacher who is active in planning and encouraging children's concept development.

Active outdoor environments for young children enhance the possibilities for learning in all curricular areas; however, natural surroundings and open spaces are especially important for building active science and math concepts. Well-planned outdoor environments invite inquiry and stimulate children's desire to find the answers to mathematical problems posed by the environment.

As mentioned previously, it is important that teachers not underestimate the influence of the learning environment on the children's experiences. When carefully planned and intentionally designed, the environment becomes another teacher, guiding children's behavior, explorations, and learning.

3

Building Connections to Home and Community Through Active Experiences

Families support mathematics learning through their activities at home, conversations, attitudes, materials they provide to their children, expectations they have about their performance, the behaviors they model, and the games they play.

National Research Council, 2010

According to the National Council of Teachers of Mathematics (2000), students, school leaders, parents, the community, and other caregivers share the responsibility to ensure that all students receive a high-quality mathematics education. When all interested parties work together in environments that are equitable, challenging, supportive, and technologically equipped, young children receive the high-quality mathematics education they will need later in school and as adults.

John Dewey believed that schools could not function "when separated from the interest of home and community" (Dewey, 1944, p. 86). He depicted the school at the center, with the free interplay of influences, materials, and ideas flowing to both the home and the environment around the school building, and back again to life in school. The work of Piaget (Youniss & Damon, 1992) and Vygotsky (Berk & Winsler, 1995) further confirms the importance of building connections to home and community through active experiences.

Vygotsky (1978) saw children as learning to think and develop concepts by mastering challenging tasks in collaboration with more knowledgeable members of their society. In addition to teachers, our communities have many specialists who are available as resources for classes and for individual students. Moreover, many communities have access to science and math centers (Lawrence Hall of Science in Berkeley, California, for example), museums, national laboratories, and industry that can contribute greatly to the understanding of math and encourage students to further their interests outside of school.

Working with others in their school and with the community, teachers will want to build these resources into their interactions with children. Through active experiences with community members, children encounter the raw materials that enable them to construct learning in the classroom that has meaning and integrity. Children are cheated when most math concepts are presented to them out of context. According to Basile (1999), one context that has proven beneficial for encouraging development of mathematical concepts and processes is the outdoor environment. Mathematics abounds in nature, and many things found there can be used to teach mathematics in a meaningful and authentic way.

In his ecological approach, Bronfenbrenner (1979) placed the developing child in the center of a series of interlocking settings. Home, school, and the neighborhood serve as the immediate basis for child development and learning. Just as active children derive meaning from their experiences in the classroom, that meaning is extended and broadened when teachers recognize the family and the community as resources for deep and personally meaningful learning experiences.

OUT INTO THE SCHOOL

Now, where can the teacher and children find the active experiences that build connections to home and community and take them outside the classroom walls?

Whether a Head Start program or grade 1 in a large elementary school, a child-care center or a small cooperative nursery school, there are many meaningful ways to utilize the immediate environment of the building itself or the grounds that surround it.

Inside the School Building

There are many possibilities for children's active math experiences when they take a walk around the school building. Patterns are everywhere in the school building, as are opportunities to measure and compare using traditional and nontraditional tools. At the Center for Young Children at the University of Maryland, a group of children went in search of patterns. They found repeated patterns on cushions, the tile floor, and the pattern bracelets created by the children in the kindergarten. They also found that the cloth holder for take-home messages had been specifically designed so that the first row had a repeated pattern of two red, two yellow, two red, two yellow. The next row had two blue, two green, two blue, two green—and the bottom row had two purple, two pink, two purple, two pink.

Children can also count the number of classrooms, tiles on the floor, windows, and doors. They can note where symbols are used and make guesses as to their meanings. When walking through the halls, they are navigating space and applying ideas about direction and distance. "Go right" and "Go left" begin to take on meaning as children practice finding their way around the building and look for landmarks and locations.

Maps can be constructed of the school building using both concrete manipulatives and drawings, although it is not expected that they will be true to scale. Teachers can create treasure hunts to give children practice in finding their way around the building using various landmarks.

The teacher should speak with community members within the school building beforehand to determine if there are opportunities to learn from them about the specific mathematical skills required to do their jobs. For example, the school nurse uses a scale to take children's weight and a thermometer for their temperature, a janitor keeps records of supplies and uses that information to order new supplies and then organizes the supplies to make them easier to locate, the office secretary sorts mail into individual staff mailboxes, and the cafeteria staff use the daily lunch count to determine how much food to make for lunch. When children return to the class, they can think about similar skills used to organize the materials in their room and may consider further how all members of the school community use math to support the school's functioning on a daily basis.

Outside in the Natural Environment

The immediate outdoor environment of the school provides children with a rich laboratory for studying nature and the physical world as it applies to mathematics. The natural world is filled with items that can be explored for the math concepts they express. There are many opportunities to consider symmetry, pattern, shape, and comparison of measurable attributes among natural items. Rocks can be sorted, classified, and ordered by size, number, and other properties. Differences in the rocks' weight can be considered, and they may be brought inside for weighing. Spiderwebs and flower petals can be used to study patterns, and trees can be measured around with string and compared as to size (and, for older children, age). Human-made structures also may be observed and considered for their expressions of the same concepts.

Teachers will enjoy finding ways to teach mathematics in a contextual format that is as authentic as possible. Through hands-on manipulation, children discover that some things are heavy and others are light, count how many berries are on a bush, and consider whether the number of spots is the same on each wing of a ladybug. These are math experiences that they will not forget and will be able to reflect on and use later when engaged in other similar experiences.

OUT INTO THE NEIGHBORHOOD AND COMMUNITY

In planning for meaningful experiences for children, teachers prepare the children, but they also prepare themselves. The purpose of a trip into the neighborhood or community is to provide children with firsthand experiences that they might be unable to have in the classroom, in school, or on the immediate grounds and to expose children to authentic uses for mathematics in the real world. In fact, the first step for the teacher might be to decide whether the purpose could be accomplished in any other way. Trips outside the classroom often require a great amount of work from both the teacher and other staff and volunteers and should be used when it is clear they will enhance experiences for children, encourage them to consider math concepts in a way they may not in the classroom, or inspire children to explore concepts in more depth in the classroom on returning from the trip. The teacher decides on the goals and then plans for experiences before, during, and after the field trip.

Teachers will want to become familiar with the community and its resources before planning any trip. Unforeseen difficulties can be avoided if teachers preview the sites and talk with the people at the places they wish to visit. Some sites, such as museums and libraries, have prepared tours and materials for children; however, these may be too long or complex for the younger children. Teachers should shorten and modify an experience when necessary and create their own materials that will be age appropriate. The box on page 34 lists some safety tips to consider when planning a field experience.

Teachers will also want to consider the integrative power of a field trip (Seefeldt, 1997). How will the math trip facilitate growth in science, the language arts, literacy, the arts, and social skills? As teachers prepare the children, they will emphasize active experiences in all of these areas. In addition, they will choose children's literature that integrates math throughout the early childhood curriculum. Each active experience will involve learning new vocabulary words and investigating the site through informational books and fiction. Before the trip, children will be encouraged to think about what their current knowledge is—what they know about the place or topic they will be exploring, what their previous experiences may have been, and what questions they would like to have answered. After the trip, they will want to organize their experiences by drawing pictures, dictating stories, making charts and graphs, and reading more stories related to the trip. They will re-create and reinvent their learnings through dramatic play inside and outside the classroom. Social skills develop as children experience new people and places and acquire behaviors to fit the situation.

SOME SAFETY TIPS FOR FIELD EXPERIENCES

- Obtain parental permission for children to participate in the excursion.
- Be sure all teachers and staff members are trained in first aid and CPR. Include at least one person with such training on the trip.
- Take a first-aid kit on the excursion.
- Take an up-to-date list of emergency phone numbers for each child.
- Check medical forms for children's allergies.
- Always walk on the left side of the street, facing traffic.
- When utilizing transportation, make sure the children know, have practiced, and will follow the rules.
- Consider the adult–child ratios. Include no more than three or four children on a field trip for each adult present, and fewer if the trip requires complex arrangements for transportation.
- Remember that small group excursions may be best for all learners.
- Be sure that the field trip site meets guidelines for children with identified disabilities. Make sure chaperones understand the unique physical or behavioral needs of individual children.

Basic Guidelines for Meaningful Field Experiences

1. Keep the experience simple for very young children and increase the complexity as it is developmentally appropriate. For example, very young children will profit from a short walk to look at repeated patterns on historical buildings. With the teacher's help, they may classify the shapes by type or use blocks of similar shapes in the block area to build structures. Older children will advance their concepts of shape and pattern by drawing or tracing what they see on the buildings and labeling the shapes and patterns, and they may be interested in comparing and contrasting the architectural features of buildings.

2. If the classroom is inclusive, consider all aspects of the field experience. Pathways and sites must be barrier free and experiences must be open-ended so that all children profit from the field trip. Some children may need more time to prepare for learning in a new environment with unfamiliar stimuli, and teachers may want to think ahead of rooms, materials, or activities that may be difficult for children with certain cognitive or emotional disabilities. Small group excursions may provide a better opportunity for all learners to profit.

3. Introduce the field experience through discussions, pictures, reading about things to be viewed, art experiences, and classroom experiments. For example, if children are to visit the grocery store, provide many books for them (both fiction and nonfiction) about stores and the things they sell. With the teacher's help, older children can make a list of things they wish to purchase, research how much the items cost, and estimate whether they have enough money to pay for them. Ask questions: "How many do we need?" "How much do you think the oranges will cost?" "How many oranges are in a dozen?" "How many bananas do you think are in a bunch?" At the Center for Young Children, one class went to PetSmart to buy supplies for classroom pets. They made a list before the trip, and small groups explored the store to find one item from the list and purchase it.

4. Organize play around the places visited. The creative dramatic center and the outside environment can be adapted to fit math field experiences. Often, additional clothes or props will be needed. Boxes and bags can fill the grocery store, along with empty cartons, cans, and bins for holding various groceries. Food scales will enhance the experience, as will aprons for the grocers and money for transactions. Cash registers with money encourage children to think about numbers and quantities that have meaning. Small groups of children can work together to classify the foods by type and then decide on fair prices. For example, different containers of milk might require different prices depending on their size or the amount of liquid they hold.

5. Prepare the children to observe closely and gather data during the field trip. Their observations will be used as the basis for many activities in the days and weeks to follow. For example, children have probably been to the grocery store with their parents many times. Yet, they have not paid close attention to the patterns, colors, shapes, and variety of goods. For older children, questions may be compiled on sheets before the trip to remind them of the things they wanted to look for.

6. Give children plenty of opportunities to reflect on their experiences. Allot time and materials for follow-up plans and projects. Isolated experiences do not allow children to explore concepts in depth or consider concepts in a variety of contexts. Reflecting on experiences through pictures, writing, and collaborating to create class books allows children to revisit their thoughts and ideas at later times. Geist (2003) suggests that when children work on projects, a number of opportunities arise for them to

Teachers help children document their field experiences in ways that support mathematical thinking.

use math. In a recent project on construction and transportation, children had an opportunity to use measurement to help them build a truck. They measured how long, tall, and wide they wanted it and then transferred their numbers to the cardboard they were using to make their truck. Their measurements were not totally accurate, but this experience served as a meaningful exploration and use of measurement concepts.

7. Encourage parents to participate during any phase of the planning, implementation, or follow-up. Opportunities for parent participation should accommodate parents' schedules. Parents need not come to the school or field experience. Teachers send home lists of materials that can be donated to support math experiences in the classroom. There are also many ways parents can enhance their children's experiences at home if the teacher communicates regularly with them regarding math plans and activities at school.

BUILDING CONNECTIONS WITH THE NEIGHBORHOOD AND COMMUNITY

The U.S. Department of Education, in its comprehensive guide for parents, *Helping Your Child Learn Mathematics*, provides activities for children ages preschool through fifth grade. These activities include experiences at home and in the community, with suggestions for thinking about math at the grocery store and "on the go" in the car or when using public transportation. The guide also provides resources such as Web sites and books for parents and children, as well as recommendations for children's software that encourages mathematical thinking. These resources are valuable for teachers, too, as they build community connections to foster children's skills in mathematics. Every community has natural resources, people resources, and material resources. Teachers and parents will want to make an effort to become acquainted with these resources to extend and expand the mathematics offerings possible in the school as well as at home.

The Neighborhood as a Mathematics Laboratory

On walking excursions out into their community, young children do best in small groups. Planning is essential when the trip is known ahead of time. The following criteria provide for experiences with integrity and meaning:

- There should be a continuity of experience as one builds on another. Build experiences around one theme or concept area—such as geometry—and help children to construct in-depth knowledge and generalize it to other areas.

- Each experience should be worth the children's and teacher's time and effort. A trip to a university math laboratory may long and exhausting, with exhibits placed too high for most children to see and touch and not engaging enough to keep their interest. When asked what they remember about the trip, they may talk about the leaves they saw on the walk over or how many steps there were leading into the building. Remember to follow what is interesting to children and consider ahead of time how the planned experiences will connect to what children are already finding new and engaging.

- Advance organizers should be provided for the children. Young children need opportunities to discuss, read about, and anticipate the excursion in advance. Some teachers find that asking children to make a list of what they already know, what they want to see, and what they think they will see on the trip is helpful.

Teachers sometimes add the question "What surprised you about the trip?" There are several varieties of KWL charts (What I **Know**—What I **Want** to know—What I **Learned**—What I still want to know) that teachers can construct. The first half is used to plan for the experience, and the second half is used to reflect on and document the trip and to plan for future experiences.

- Children should have time to reflect on experiences outside the classroom and follow up with plans and projects that enhance and expand their learning. For example, after a trip to the post office, the children were interested in developing their own system for getting mail from one part of the school to another. They realized that the different rooms in the school were not identified by number, meaning that mail might not get to its intended destination. They developed a system for numbering the rooms and decided it was important for delivery purposes that the mail first be sorted into two groups—for the two different hallways of the building—and then delivered.

- A planned experience should either be an outgrowth of children's deep interests or meet a specific need for the children in learning subject matter content. Mrs. Porter's class became very interested in the patterns and shapes they observed in art and in the classroom itself. They were excited when their teacher extended their experiences by taking them to a craft store where many different types of patterns were available to observe. Each child was able to choose a pattern that was appealing, and the store owner donated many different scraps of material to take back to school to use in the art area.

- Flexibility is essential. Although most outside experiences are planned in advance, children may express interest in things the teacher may not have considered, such as the numbers counting down on the walk/don't walk sign, or the shadows the children make along the way. These observations lead to new questions and investigations and give teachers the opportunity to utilize all areas of the math curriculum for young children.

Neighborhood Resources

Local Businesses

Teachers need to identify people who are knowledgeable about how math is used in their business and like to talk to young children. It is nice if hands-on experiences are available as well. A restaurant or small store is a good place to learn basic concepts such as classification, weight, and how numbers are related to quantity and price. With the teacher's help, children can make a grocery list, count out money, and go to the store to buy the ingredients for a cooking project or a party. They can set up a grocery store in the classroom, organizing shelves by type of food and deciding on prices for food. Older elementary children may be interested in how much it costs to buy the food and pay the employees and may wonder how prices are determined. They can also be allocated an amount of money to buy lunch at a neighborhood restaurant and make sure they do not spend more than they have.

Buildings and Houses in the Community

Houses and other buildings can contribute to children's thinking about math concepts. Young children notice large differences in height and may identify basic shapes such as rectangles and squares. They may represent what they have observed through drawings in the art area or with block structures. Older children can consider more complex ideas such as architectural similarities as well as community design and create their own communities or building designs with two- or three-dimensional displays.

Maps

Making and using maps involves measurement, geometry, and a great deal of spatial thinking. According to Ginsburg and Amit (2008), creating maps includes the use of six specific mathematical concepts. The first is *representation*, requiring children to think about and represent reality through the abstract. The second is *projection*, which is the ability to represent three-dimensional space through a two-dimensional image. An understanding of *proportion* is necessary so that representations on the map are drawn to scale, and *1–1 correspondence* ensures that each physical item is represented only once on the map. *Approximation and coding* allow for representations that clearly identify objects even without an exact drawing of the item and standardized codes, such as a break in the line of the wall to represent a door. Finally, *rotation of plane* is necessary for reading a map that is in a different orientation than the space represented (e.g., looking at a map placed vertically on the wall requires mental rotation in order to navigate the horizontal floor represented). Young children can make simple maps that will not be proportionately accurate but may demonstrate some beginning understanding that three-dimensional space can be represented in a two-dimensional way. Working with the teacher's guidance, they can choose shapes to represent furniture, windows, or doors. This is the beginning of symbolic representation.

Science Centers and Museums

These facilities have planned activities for children, including experiments and opportunities to use technology that small preschools and most elementary schools cannot afford. At the Lawrence Hall of Science in Berkeley, California, there is a program called Family Math in which families work together on math concepts and problems. Family Math has been expanded to other areas of the country as well. At the Smithsonian Institution in Washington, D.C., "Don't Touch" has been replaced by "Please Touch with Care" in the discovery and interactive computer areas of the museum. In Philadelphia, Pennsylvania, the Please Touch Museum encourages children to be actively engaged in their learning, using all of their senses to explore math and science concepts.

The Zimmerli Art Museum at Rutgers University provides opportunities for children to observe art in the context of music and storytelling and then to express their understanding of the story and music through art. Through these art experiences, children develop spatial thinking skills—learning to fill spaces on a piece of paper in different ways—as well as appreciation for patterns, shape, and geometry in art.

Other Community Resources

Teachers may also want to consider these community resources:

- Colleges and universities
- Radio or television stations
- Professional services such as doctors' offices and hospitals
- Commercial services such as bakeries, pharmacies, markets, factories, farms, shoe repair shops, and hardware stores
- Children's museums with hands-on exhibits

Visitors to the classroom who contribute to the math curriculum include parents and other specialists in computer technologies, music, art, cooking, mechanics, and many other fields that have mathematics aspects. They can be effective resource people if the teacher prepares the children carefully for their visits and encourages visitors to provide active demonstrations or hands-on opportunities.

The Home–School Connection

> Parents (including, for our purposes in this book, adult family members and other caregivers), especially of young children, want to be involved in their children's education. Their ideas of how to help usually include reading to their children, helping them learn the alphabet, and teaching them how to count. Frequently, however, parents don't know how to go beyond these activities, especially in mathematics. (Davila Coates & Thompson, 1999, p. 205)

Classrooms work best and children learn more when parents are involved. The joint position statement of the National Association for the Education of Young Children and the National Council for Teachers of Mathematics (2002) suggests public campaigns to build awareness of the family's central role in mathematical development. It is also possible to distribute materials in ways similar to those of reading initiatives and to provide computer-linked as well as school-based meetings for families. Teachers may employ the following multiple approaches, as well as modeling some of their strategies from the Family Math after-school family involvement program, which has worked since 1981 to involve parents and caregivers of kindergarten to grade 8 children in their mathematics education:

• **Conferences.** These meetings are an opportunity for teachers to provide parents with samples of children's work. Teachers can also invite parents to share their observations about their children's learning and discuss what will be coming next in their development of certain skills. Teachers ask parents if their children show interest in math concepts at home and provide suggestions for helping them continue to explore areas of interest.

• **Meetings and workshops.** Family Math found that a huge number of adults had inaccurate concepts of what math teaching was all about and felt at a loss to begin to work on math concepts with their children. Some of the ideas in part Two will assist teachers in giving parents the confidence to explore math with their children. In addition, math concepts should be taught in the child's (and parent's) native language whenever possible. Many books for children that encourage mathematical thinking have been translated into Spanish and other languages, including *The Doorbell Rang (Llaman a la Puerta)* by Pat Hutchins and *Moja Means One: Swahili Counting Book* by Muriel Feelings.

• **Informal contacts.** Busy parents enjoy a brief chat before school, telephone calls, informal notes or e-mails, and bulletin boards or Web sites that inform them of plans and programs and invite them to participate in a variety of ways. At one urban preschool program, many children walked to school each day with other children from the community, so the teacher was not able to speak with parents regularly. She found that because of the parents' busy work schedules, phone calls were difficult to arrange. After establishing appropriate boundaries and rules, she began using cell phone text messages to communicate with parents about activities at school and discovered that parents were extremely responsive and increasingly engaged.

• **Formal contacts.** Somewhat more formal contacts through the provision of a Parents' Corner or Family Room give parents a chance to interact around math learning materials, reference books, children's literature based on math, and other activities of interest to the family. Often these items may be checked out by family members.

• **Newsletters.** Regular communications explain the goals for the week, why certain activities were planned, and how parents can support the lessons at home. Each active experience in part Two of this book has a section that explains what parents can do in an informal way to support children's emergent concept development in the area of math. Other items to include in newsletters are special events at school, math activities and puzzles that children have enjoyed, special television programs on topics of math that parents and children might watch together, and special events for children and families occurring in the community. Newsletters should be short, sweet, and to the point if teachers hope for parents to read them. Keep them simple and informative, and write them in a way that will be accessible to all parents. If there are children whose parents speak another language, keep the language very simple or find someone to translate the newsletter. If a translator is not available, there are now some rather sophisticated translation options available online, such as http://translate. google.com.

• **Open-door policy with frequent invitations.**   Such a policy provides opportunities for parent observation and participation. Parents should feel welcome in the classroom, to stay in the morning to participate in greeting routines, to come eat lunch with a child, or to stop by and observe or participate in activities. If parents are unable to work regularly as paid or unpaid volunteers, they may make or send materials for special projects in the classroom, help on field experiences, or come to school when their schedules permit.

• **Parties and meetings.**   Informal gatherings, such as Family Math Nights, give parents an opportunity to ask questions and have hands-on experiences themselves with the math curriculum being used in the classroom. Parents will enjoy playing teacher or child-made math games, working puzzles, or creating with geoboards, tangrams, or pattern blocks. One of the goals of the Family Math program is to get families talking together about mathematical ideas and doing activities that sometimes involve informal learning centers. In addition, this is an opportunity for teachers to model appropriate language and interactions that support children's learning.

• **Take-home papers.**   Active math experiences for children can be documented for parents. Children will have products such as drawings, charts, or stories to communicate to busy parents what they are doing in school. It is important that these products often be accompanied by explanations from teachers explaining what math concepts have been explored and suggesting follow-up questions or activities that can be done at home.

Parents can encourage children to think mathematically by asking open-ended questions and taking time to encourage the answers. They can help their children to observe ("What shapes do you see on that tree?"), classify ("Let's put away your toys by color"), and quantify ("How many steps did we take to get down to the subway?"). It is possible to practice the skills of mathematics everywhere.

Teachers will want to plan family math events at school and include suggestions in the class newsletter for supporting math learning in the home—such as a simple recipe that requires measurement. Successful school math events will involve the whole family in collecting data, undertaking the investigation of problems, and solving math puzzles. These are active experiences for the whole family; when children and parents work together on math, parents learn math, too.

The following interactions with parents should introduce them to, and involve them in, children's mathematics experiences:

1. In the class newsletter, have a weekly suggestion box designed to supplement the math curriculum at home. For example, highlight free activities occurring in the community, such as children's book readings at libraries or bookstores, exhibits to be visited, and activities based on kitchen and gardening math. Suggest conversation starters around math concepts, such as "I wonder how many . . ." or "How were the shapes we found on our walk the same/different?"

2. Put together a "math backpack" that children take home on a rotating basis. The backpack contains a note explaining the purpose of the activity, an information book or story related to the activity, and all the materials necessary for completing the activity. The teacher will want to make sure that all of the materials contained in the backpack are easy and fun for parents and children to use and are translated into the child's home language if possible.

3. Compile a list of Web sites that specifically target parents and math—such as the "Figure This!" math challenges from the National Council of Teachers of Mathematics and Sesame Workshop's "Math Is Everywhere." Many public libraries offer access to computers for families who do not own them. The teacher should make sure that all families who want to take advantage of online activities have a way to do so. Investigate whether there are applications for smartphones that are appropriate for preschool children and encourage mathematical thinking.

In addition, even if family members cannot volunteer in the classroom on a regular basis, they can share their talents, occupations, hobbies, customs, and traditions with the class and school community as they are able. Juan's father loved to build furniture. He shared his talents with the class, demonstrating how he used standard measuring tools and providing scraps of materials with guidance for planning and building. From this experience, the children understood that math is important in all endeavors.

SUMMARY

According to Davila Coates and Thompson (1999), working with community members and using community settings are often effective ways of reaching parents who have traditionally been alienated from the schools. Libraries, community centers, and community-based organizations can serve as alternative venues. Choosing mathematics activities that parents recognize as important to them is also significant in getting parents to buy into the math program.

Building and maintaining connections with home and community provides benefits to all. Young children need active experiences consistent with but expanding on their participation in mathematics education. These experiences require careful planning by teachers, who are rewarded by observing children's authentic learning as one experience builds on another into an integrated whole. When the family is recognized as a valuable resource for learning, parents and teachers feel mutually supported and learn to understand and value each other as contributors to the child's understanding of mathematics. All of this is consistent with a strong emphasis on mathematics in the curriculum for young children.

4

Connecting Everyday Experiences with Mathematical Content

Experiences, in order to be educative, must lead out into an expanding world of subject-matter.

John Dewey, 1938

Children have firsthand experiences and investigations with mathematics before they even begin formal schooling. The mathematical concepts and problems they encounter daily in their classrooms, homes, and communities form the foundation for success in future math learning. Children gain mathematical knowledge as they notice that they are taller or shorter than a brother or sister, as they count fruits to put in a bag at the grocery, and as they grapple with the problem of how to balance a block tower or share a bowl of grapes with several friends.

These informal ideas of math, however, are only the first rungs on the learning ladder. They help children make sense of their world and help them construct a solid foundation for success in school (NAEYC & NCTM, 2002). The next step on the learning ladder is the expansion and extension of the knowledge children have gained through their firsthand experiences into a fuller, richer, deeper, and more organized form (Dewey, 1938; NAEYC & NCTM, 2002). This form gradually approximates the experts' understanding of mathematics.

According to Sarama and Clements (2006), children's potential for learning mathematics is not well realized. They point to the fact that even before starting kindergarten, most children in the United States know substantially less about math than do children from other countries. Further, children from "low-resource" communities have the least knowledge of any group studied, and there is an urgent need to bring excellent teachers and resources to these children.

Teachers who enable children to turn their direct, firsthand experiences with their world into a coherent, organized body of mathematical knowledge are the double specialists described by Piaget (1970). These are teachers who are engrossed in knowledge of each individual child—what each child knows, how each one learns—and who also have knowledge of the subject matter of mathematics. Then, because teachers are double specialists, they are better prepared to bring children and subject matter content together. Much of understanding mathematics concepts lies in the connections between ideas. Teachers need to help children to connect their considerable informal knowledge to their budding explicit knowledge of mathematics.

KNOWLEDGE OF CHILDREN

Knowledge of children and their typical cognitive and mathematical developmental trajectories is necessary for planning appropriate and meaningful experiences. There will be wide variations in development due to the sociocultural context of children's lives and the variation in patterns of normal growth and development. Even though individual children develop differently, research and theory inform us about how children's cognitive development and mathematical understanding typically occur. Jean Piaget (1970) studied children's thinking and their concepts of number. He outlined the development of number concepts in children, tracing the beginning of number concepts from birth at the sensorimotor stage through formal operations at around age 11 or 12. Since that time, researchers have continued to investigate what children know and are capable of doing in the early years. Ginsburg (2006, 2009); Ginsburg, Pappas, and Seo (2001); Clements and Sarama (2006, 2009); Starkey, Klein, and Wakely (2004); and Sarama et al. (2008) have contributed in different ways to the field of knowledge regarding children's math abilities, teaching, and assessment. The research includes many forms of assessment, from observation, to short tasks, to longer "flexible interviews" (Ginsburg, 2009), to more formal, standardized assessments. From these assessments, children demonstrate that they follow fairly predictable patterns of development in their understanding of number sense, geometry, measurement, and pattern.

University of Buffalo researchers Douglas H. Clements and Julie Sarama have documented these trajectories in a guide for teachers in their book *Learning and Teaching Early Math: The Learning Trajectories Approach* (Clements & Sarama, 2009). This guide provides teachers with resources for understanding children's developmental trajectories from birth to age 8, along with recommendations for assessment and teaching. By better understanding how children's knowledge develops, teachers are better prepared to provide meaningful learning experiences and can be more effective in their instruction.

KNOWLEDGE OF THE SUBJECT MATTER: MATHEMATICS

Knowledge of children's development alone is not enough. If teachers are to guide children as they move further up the learning ladder, then teachers must also have a solid understanding of the subject matter they want children to learn and a repertoire of strategies to teach it.

Just as authorities in the field of early childhood have identified universals of children's growth, development, and learning, so have authorities in the field of mathematics identified general facts, information, and knowledge that are key to mathematics (NCTM, 2000). Knowledge of these key concepts that organize mathematical content guides teachers as they select firsthand experiences that will serve as a base for children's learning. In addition, teachers can lead children in expanding and extending these firsthand experiences into more formal, conventional knowledge.

Principles for Teaching Mathematics

The National Council of Teachers of Mathematics (1989, 2000, 2002, 2006) has established principles for teaching mathematics to children. These principles of learning are embedded in the standards.

Equity

The National Council of Teachers of Mathematics supports the idea that all children and their families hold high expectations for children's mathematical learning and that these expectations are fulfilled through strong support, curriculum, and programs for all of our nation's children. In its position statement *The Mathematics Education of Underrepresented Groups* (2002), the NCTM stated its commitment to the principle that groups underrepresented in mathematics-based fields of study—African Americans, Hispanics/Latinos, Native Americans, Alaskan Natives, Pacific Islanders, females, children in poor communities, children with disabilities, and Asian Americans, among others—should be full participants in all aspects of mathematics education.

The recommendations for inclusive practices include the following:

- Teachers should motivate and encourage every student to continue the study of mathematics.

- Schools and districts should examine and correct policies, programs, and practices that may lead to mathematics avoidance.

- Mathematics educators should make an individual and collective commitment to eliminate any psychological and institutional barriers to the study of mathematics.

- Educators should explore and implement effective ways to convince students and families from underrepresented groups of the importance of mathematics as a viable field of study.

Curriculum

Teachers understand that mathematics learning is not a series of isolated one-time activities, but rather is a coherent, focused, and well-articulated program that continues from early childhood through the grades (NAEYC & NCTM, 2002). Most recently, the NCTM's *Curriculum Focal Points for Prekindergarten Through Grade 8 Mathematics* (2006) focuses on a few broad concepts or "targets" for each grade level. The emphasis is on depth and problem solving. Fortunately, over the past few years, several research-based mathematics curricula for young children have been developed that are focused on improving young children's knowledge and skills.

- The *Big Math for Little Kids* curriculum (Balfanz, Ginsburg, & Greenes, 2003; Ginsburg, Greenes, & Balfanz, 2003) engages children through activities and storybooks and guides them sequentially through concepts such as number, shape, pattern, measurement, operations on number, and space.

- The *High/Scope* curriculum (Hohmann & Weikart, 2002) has recently released *Numbers Plus,* which focuses on number as well as shape, space, measurement, algebra, and data analysis. The curriculum includes training and resources for teachers, including learning trajectories for each activity.

- *Building Blocks* (Clements & Sarama, 2007a) is based on an extensive body of research on developmental trajectories and integrates three types of media: computers, manipulatives, and print. The focus of the curriculum is on space and geometry and numbers and quantity. Research has demonstrated gains for children from low-SES families (Clements & Sarama, 2007b, c).

- The *Number Worlds* curriculum (Griffin, 2007b) builds children's understanding of basic number concepts from preschool through the sixth grade. The focus of the program is to connect the many uses of numbers in our world and provides activities meant to engage children's imaginations.

Teaching

Knowing mathematics means "doing mathematics." As stated by NCTM: "A person gathers, discovers, or creates knowledge in the course of some activity having a purpose" (1989, p. 7). Thus, both teaching and learning mathematics, not just for young children but for adults as well, emphasize firsthand experiences that involve students in meaningful, purposeful activity. This is an area of concern in teacher preparation programs, because few 2- or 4-year undergraduate early childhood programs provide adequate mathematics instruction (Ginsburg, Lee, & Boyd, 2008).

Technology

With the advent of computers and other technology, many aspects of doing mathematics have changed in the last decade. This does not mean, however, that children do not need opportunities to develop an understanding of mathematical models, structures, and simulations applicable to many disciplines.

The mathematics program in childhood should take advantage of technology. According to the National Research Council (2010), computer use is a valid way for children to manipulate shapes and even "may have some specific advantages" (p. 196). For example, there are more possibilities for manipulating, composing, and decomposing shapes on the computer than with actual physical shapes. Manipulations can be saved and revisited or reflected on, and computer programs can do some things that are more difficult or impossible to do with physical materials, such as creating three-dimensional block structures that do not fall down, cutting a 3D shape in half, drawing a symmetrical shape to match the shape the child has created, and automatically providing appropriately more challenging activities when a child demonstrates understanding. With a teacher's guidance, children can engage in exciting and challenging activities made possible with new technology.

Teachers should also use available technology to simplify and enhance assessment practices. New assessment tools are available that allow teachers to record and organize observations, anecdotes, and work samples. For example, the Early Learning Scale (Riley-Ayers, Stevenson-Garcia, Frede, & Breneman, 2009) is a comprehensive, standards-based assessment system that allows teachers to collect data on handheld devices and synchronize automatically to an online program that organizes data and automatically produces portfolios and parent-friendly summaries of children's development.

Learning

Piaget and Inhelder (1969) demonstrated that children construct their own knowledge through their social, mental, and physical activities.

To foster children's construction of mathematics knowledge, teachers will need to determine what children already know about mathematics and what they still have to learn. Children's development of math concepts should move through increasingly sophisticated levels of constructing ideas and skills.

Time, appropriate materials, and interaction with others are necessary to support children's engagement in mathematical ideas. Play is the way children can pursue their own purposes and tackle problems that are challenging and yet within their own capabilities (NAEYC & NCTM, 2002).

Mathematics is integrated with other learning activities, and other learning activities are integrated with mathematics. Children learn about mathematics and learn to apply mathematical thinking through everyday activities. For example, children use egg timers to take turns with popular toys, they figure out how many place settings are needed at lunch if three children are absent, and they learn about measurement and space when putting materials back on a shelf and realizing that a basket is too large to fit in a particular spot.

Problem Solving

Focus on problem solving. Problem solving and reasoning are the heart of mathematics (NAEYC & NCTM, 2002). Therefore, children are encouraged to observe, question, collect information, communicate ideas, make connections and representations, and reflect on their experiences. Problems should arise from children's authentic experiences. For example, children in a Head Start program in New Mexico were interested in making blankets out of scrap materials for the babies in the dramatic play area. There were two baby cribs of different sizes, and two different-sized blankets were needed. The teacher wondered out loud with the children how they could make sure the blankets were the right size. This led to several attempts and failures, including the incorrect application of a measuring tape. Finally, the children created construction paper "patterns" that were then pinned to the material before cutting.

Children can document problem-solving strategies with dry-erase boards.

Assessment

Authentic assessment is an integral part of the teaching-learning cycle. It is intentional and guided by standards, connected to children's individual skills, and informs planning and instruction. As children build with blocks, teachers note their use of descriptive shape words, their spatial thinking and attention to symmetry, and their use of classification skills to put blocks away on the correct shelves. While children play games, teachers observe them as they count how many spaces to move or match numbers or symbols. Assessment can be complex and controversial, but in the early years it should be authentic and formative, used to learn more about children's learning and to prepare for more effective instruction.

It is not safe to assume that because a child is playing with counting bears, he is actually exploring concepts of counting. It is the role of the teacher to ask questions that will help demonstrate the thinking taking place. Teachers enhance children's mathematical reasoning by asking questions that require thoughtful responses. By responding to the mathematical ideas that have come about in children's play, teachers are more likely to engage students in a conversation regarding those ideas (NCTM, 2000). Encouraging children to talk about their observations, thoughts, and reasoning helps them to develop their communication skills, to become flexible in their thinking, and to become more reflective (Copley, 2000).

NCTM Standards

The standards that the National Council of Teachers of Mathematics has delineated are not separate topics or themes; they are interwoven strands designed to support the learning of meaningful mathematics. These standards include the targeted focal points discussed next. Suggestions for including them in the curriculum are presented in Part Two of this book.

1. Number and Operations

At the heart of mathematics is an understanding of numbers. Children need to be able to make sense of the ways numbers are used in their everyday world (NCTM, 1989). They will begin with counting—and as they mature and have increasingly sophisticated experiences, they will count with understanding, knowing that when they count four objects, four is the number of objects they have.

Children will begin to find ways of representing numbers. They may make marks, or begin to recognize and write numerals. Children will also begin to understand the meanings of number operations and how they relate to one another. Involved in real-life experiences, children begin to ask questions about number operations: "How many are left?" "How many more do we need?" "How many did you add?"

2. Algebra

Children identify, duplicate, and extend simple number patterns and sequential and growing patterns (patterns made with shapes) as preparation for creating rules that describe relationships. Expectations for children include the following:

- Sorting, classifying, and ordering objects by size, number, and other properties

- Recognizing, describing, and extending patterns such as sequences of sound and shape

- Using concrete, pictorial, and verbal representations to develop an understanding of symbolic notations

- Describing qualitative and quantitative changes, such as changes in colors, textures, appearance (qualitative) and numbers, measurement, cost (quantitative).

A component of algebra, *patterning*, "merits special mention because it is accessible and interesting to young children" (NAEYC & NCTM, 2002, p. 9). Being able to recognize, describe, and create patterns undergirds algebraic thinking and supports the development of number sense, spatial sense, and other conceptual areas. Pattern recognition involves all kinds of things. Children can begin to notice patterns in the routines of the day, patterns in music or poetry, or patterns of colors, shapes, or sizes. Being able to recognize patterns arranged in a rule-governed manner leads to recognizing a variety of relationships, which in turn leads to making mathematical connections (NCTM, 1989).

3. Geometry and Spatial Awareness

Geometry is another area of particular importance in the curriculum for young children and into the early primary years. Young children's natural awareness of shapes and space and their manipulation of various shapes develops into more sophisticated vocabulary that includes identifying and describing—as well as being able to compare and contrast—the various attributes of two- and three-dimensional shapes.

Geometry also involves spatial awareness and understanding. To develop spatial awareness, children need to investigate, experiment with, and explore everyday objects and physical materials. They should be able to tell or represent position (where) and direction (which way). They need to feel themselves in space, climbing high, swinging low, crawling in and out of objects, on top of and under other objects. They also require opportunities to put together and take apart different shapes. As children do so, teachers introduce them to the vocabulary of space, question them about their position in space, and help them relate ideas of shapes and space to number concepts and measurement.

4. Measurement

Measurement is a common way for children to explore numbers and patterns, and early experiences provide a background for children's future understanding of volume, weight, distance, and so forth. Before children can understand measurable attributes, they must have firsthand experiences using arbitrary tools such as string or blocks to measure things and spaces in their world. Children learn to compare and estimate magnitude and quantities, although their early understanding is limited by their cognitive development. They focus largely on the visual to make comparisons. It is only later that they develop the ability to think beyond the visual to concepts such as volume, density, and quantity. From their many early experiences with informal measurement, children will eventually develop needs for conventional measurement.

5. Data Description, Organization, Representation, and Analysis

Active children learn through active experiences. Teachers demonstrate for children how their real-life experiences and investigations can be organized, represented, displayed, and reflected on with various kinds of graphs, pictures, and words to document investigations and their results. Children draw and paint pictures to represent their work, discuss problems encountered, reflect on former solutions, and reach conclusions or begin new investigations.

6. Problem Solving

Children seem driven to solve problems. They explore and examine their world—tasting, taking things apart, pulling, pushing—all in an attempt to find out how it works. This natural drive to solve problems is the foundation of the mathematics program. Teachers make certain that children will encounter many real-life mathematical problems. These will arise from both real-world and mathematical contexts (NCTM, 1989).

Teachers help children represent real-life experiences in graphical form.

Curriculum Focal Points and Connections

To enable teachers to work better with the standards at various grade levels, the NCTM recently issued *Curriculum Focal Points for Prekindergarten Through grade 8 Mathematics: A Quest for Coherence* (2006). In prekindergarten through grade 3 (the ages covered by this book), there are sets of three curriculum focal points and related connections. These topics are the recommended content emphases for the grade level specified. The document affirms the position that the focal points be addressed in contexts that promote problem solving, reasoning, communication, making connections, and designing and analyzing representations.

For example, curriculum focal points for prekindergarten include these:

- **Number and operations:** Representing, comparing, and ordering whole numbers and joining and separating sets

- **Geometry:** Describing shapes and space

- **Measurement:** Ordering objects by measurable attributes

The document provides connections to data analysis, more advanced geometry, and algebra but makes clear which concepts are both important and appropriate for each grade level. The focal points and connections for each grade level through grade 3 are described in context in Part Two of this book, with suggested investigations, experiences, and activities to convey them to children.

USING KNOWLEDGE OF MATHEMATICS TO GUIDE CHILDREN'S DEVELOPMENT

Without a solid understanding of children's mathematical development, teachers are limited in helping them see and understand relationships, or make connections between numbers, measurement, and other areas of mathematics. To bring children and mathematics together, teachers first need to find out all they can about the content of mathematics and research-based expectations for children's development. To do so, they might do the following:

- Read recent publications on mathematics and early childhood. Clements and Sarama's *Learning and teaching early math: the learning trajectories approach* (2009) is an excellent resource with many examples of children's learning and suggestions for relevant activities. Position papers and journal articles can be downloaded from the Web. (See the References and Resources at the back of this book.) The NCTM publishes a journal, *Teaching Children Mathematics,* which has many interesting articles and ideas for pre-kindergarten through grade 3. Some of the activities for older children may be adapted.

- Seek out and attend lectures and workshops on the development of mathematical thinking and best teaching practices for guiding this development.

- Talk with upper-primary-grade teachers to find out what mathematics concepts children learn in the later primary grades and discuss how to best build children's foundational knowledge of these areas.

- Visit various Web sites (see References and Resources at the end of this book) to identify appropriate investigations and problem-solving activities for children. Try out commercial and teacher/child-made mathematical games and problems.

Recapture the joy experienced by children as they identify problems, devise plans, and find solutions.

- Become acquainted with all genres of children's books that can be used to help children explore mathematical concepts. The books recommended in the remaining chapters of this book not only are rewarding to read, but also clarify concepts essential to children's learning and provide the basis for many interesting mathematical activities.

Once teachers have a solid understanding of mathematics and the development of mathematical thinking, they will want to find out what children already know and understand about mathematical concepts. To do so, teachers can do the following:

- Observe children. In order for teachers to instruct most effectively, they need to first observe children to learn about what they do and do not know and how they learn (Ginsburg et al., 2009). Teachers should note how children use number concepts and ideas and how they solve mathematical problems, use their mathematical language, and interact with others using math concepts.

- Interview children. Ask children specific questions about specific concepts. For example, teachers might ask children how they can tell two shapes are the same or different, or how shapes look different when viewed in different orientations.

- Talk with children's families. Teachers can ask about family goals for children's mathematical learning and what math experiences the child is interested in and likes doing, is not familiar with, or perhaps needs to become familiar with.

EXPANDING AND EXTENDING FIRSTHAND EXPERIENCES

Before children even begin formal schooling, their experiences with the world contribute to the development of informal, everyday mathematical ideas. This everyday, personal knowledge, however, does not automatically lead to a deeper understanding or more conventional way of knowing. The richer the new information, the greater the possibility for children to see the relationship between one math fact and another and to form generalizations.

Vygotsky (1986) pointed out that at different developmental stages, children learn different things as they independently act on and interpret their environment—but other people also interact with children, affecting the course of their development and learning. Vygotsky believed that children operate at two levels of thought. One is the *actual developmental level,* which describes tasks that the child can do independently, without adult help or guidance. The second level is the *potential developmental level,* which refers to a level of problem solving that is achieved only under the guidance of an adult or more skilled peer. The distance between the two levels was termed the *zone of proximal development* (Vygotsky, 1986).

This means that by understanding children's existing ideas and their likely developmental trajectory, teachers can extend and expand children's knowledge with the following approaches:

- Provide children with all kinds of books—poetry, literature, single-concept, picture, and reference books—that include mathematics standards and concepts. Books should be openly displayed on shelves or tables, in all areas of the classroom, inviting children to extend and expand their ideas of a given concept.

Children can use some books independently; teachers should read others to the entire group and to small groups or individual children.

- Show children how they can use number operations to solve problems. Working collaboratively with children, teachers can demonstrate how to cut paper in half; share a bowl of baby carrots so each child has three carrots; set a table with one plate, napkin, and glass at each place; or cut play dough into enough pieces for everyone to have some.

- Identify numerals in meaningful contexts. Knowing the names of numerals is *social knowledge*. Social knowledge is different from abstract knowledge (Piaget & Inhelder, 1969). Social knowledge—for example, "the name of this figure is *five,* and it stands for *five* things; count *five* blocks"—is learned through experiences. When the experiences are meaningful, children will be more likely to return to the concept and use it correctly in the future.

- Question children. Asking intentional, open-ended questions spurs children's thinking in a new, different, or more conventional way. Asking how many they have, what would happen if they took two away, why they made the pattern the way they did, how they knew a shape would fit in a certain spot, and so on, leads children to thinking about their actions.

- If a computer is available, work with children on the computer to explore math concepts, learn a new skill or fact, find information, or communicate with others.

- Use the language of mathematics. Introduce words such as *more than, less than, fewer, equals or equal to, measure, taller, longer, heavier, lighter, first,* and *last.*

- Add another experience. Based on your understanding of children's ideas and concepts of mathematics, add another real-life experience or ask another relevant question that will expand and extend their learning.

- Provide multiple opportunities for children to learn from one another.

Children should be able to revisit their existing ideas of mathematics by freely sharing their view of the world with others and arguing their point of view. Only through interactions with others can children critically consider their existing ideas and revise these to form more complex and conventional concepts of their world. Teachers patiently wait for children to work through their approaches, allowing them to learn from errors or incorrect hypotheses, and encourage children to think critically about the differences among approaches to the same solution.

Respecting children, how they learn, and the subject matter, teachers extend and expand children's existing knowledge. Bredekamp and Rosegrant (1995) ask teachers "not to water down the learning experience even for the youngest child" (p. 22), but rather to build on children's existing knowledge and experience, assessing and supporting learning.

SUMMARY

Firsthand experiences enable children to construct everyday, spontaneous mathematics concepts. These concepts are the first rung on a ladder of learning. The role of the teacher is to extend and expand these concepts into fuller, richer, more formal understanding. Teachers do this by developing an understanding of children and how they learn, developing their knowledge of content, and then bringing the two together.

Concepts can be expanded and extended in a number of ways. Books, print media, the computer, and other technologies can be used intentionally to engage children. Teachers can demonstrate skills or apply concepts and give children information that will enable them to reach a fuller understanding of themselves and the world in which they live. The following checklist will assist teachers in picking quality mathematics books for young children:

CHECKLIST FOR CHOOSING MATHEMATICS BOOKS FOR YOUNG CHILDREN

- Is it a good book? Would I read this book to the children even if I were not choosing it for a math lesson?
- Is the book engaging? Will the children be inspired to begin their own authentic investigations as a result of reading this book?
- Do the children make connections with the book? Do the characters or concepts resonate with them so they are interested in exploring further?
- Are the concepts and math connections presented as a natural part of the story or nonfictional presentation?
- Does the book include repetitive phrases or rhyming patterns that allow children to retell parts of the story while reading it again independently?
- Does the author use interesting details?
- Is the book well organized with a clear structure?
- Is it easy to find information?
- Are there useful features such as an index, a table of contents, a glossary, and suggestions for other books and resources on the topic?
- Does the book have an appealing layout and design?
- Do photographs, diagrams, graphics, and other illustrations add to, explain, and extend information?
- Are the content and the language developmentally appropriate for the intended audience?

PART TWO

Guides to Active Experiences

Guides to Active Experiences

5

Developing Ideas of Number and Operations

———————————————— FOR THE TEACHER ————————————————

◇ **What You'll Need to Know**

In addition to *Principles and Standards for School Mathematics* (2000), the National Council of Teachers of Mathematics released *Curriculum Focal Points for Prekindergarten Through Grade 8 Mathematics: A Quest for Coherence* (2006). Curriculum focal points recommended for content emphasis in prekindergarten and kindergarten are discussed in the following paragraphs, as are the related expectations for prekindergarten and kindergarten considered essential for developing ideas of number and operations. Expectations through grade 3 will be highlighted at the end of the chapter in the section titled "Extending and Expanding to the Primary Grades." Each of the subsequent chapters will follow the same format.

The prekindergarten curriculum focal points for number and operations involve developing an understanding of whole numbers, including concepts of correspondence, counting, and comparison. The National Research Council (2009) emphasizes the importance of number concepts during the early childhood years by recommending that more time be spent on number than on other concepts. According to the focal points, prekindergarten children develop an understanding of the meanings of whole numbers and recognize the number of objects in small groups without counting and in larger groups by counting. The process of using numbers to quantify is the first and most basic mathematical algorithm. Initially, the number sequence is just another song children sing as they work. Eventually, they come to understand that number words refer to quantity. They use one-to-one correspondence to count objects to 10 and beyond. They count to determine amounts and compare quantities, and eventually they order sets by the number of objects in them. Typical math language for prekindergarten children includes *more than* and *less than*. Children should be encouraged to use numbers *for a purpose*, to find out how many or to solve a problem. In using the curriculum focal points for both prekindergarten and kindergarten, teachers should be sure to address them in contexts that promote problem solving, reasoning, communication, and making connections.

The content expectation for prekindergarten—numbers and operations—is to count with understanding and recognize "how many" in sets of objects.

Kindergarten curriculum focal points for number and operations are representing, comparing, and ordering whole numbers and joining and separating sets. Children use numbers to represent quantities and to solve quantitative problems, such as counting objects in a set, creating a set with a given number of objects, comparing, ordering sets or numerals, and modeling simple joining and separating situations with objects. They are capable of choosing and applying effective strategies for answering simple quantitative questions.

Related expectations for school mathematics content standards for kindergarten include the following:

- Count with understanding and recognize "how many" in sets of objects.

- Develop an understanding of the relative position and magnitude of whole numbers and of ordinal and cardinal numbers and their connections.

- Connect number words and numerals to the quantities they represent, using various physical models and representations.

For younger children, the basic elements of counting have not yet developed.

"I can count to 10," says 3-year-old Darnella. "Listen to me," she continues. "One, two, four, five, ten." During the period of infancy and toddlerhood, children begin developing mathematical skills, concepts, and misconceptions of number (NRC, 2009). By age 2, children are counting from 1 to 5 or 6 and can identify how many objects there are by subitizing (or recognizing the amount visually, without counting) up to sets of three things. Three-year-olds become more proficient at the number sequence—although, as Darnella demonstrated, much of what children know of number is limited to counting that includes frequent mistakes and missing portions in the counting sequence (Baroody & Wilkins, 1999; NRC, 2001).

Because children count fingers and buttons and sign and chant finger-plays involving counting to 10, adults may think that early counting is a simple process for them. Yet, young children's counting is not simple, but a highly complex process. Repeating the counting sequence requires simple memorization. But beyond that, the process of counting to find quantity involves thinking, perception, and movement (NRC, 2001). To be able to count, children must think, "What is being counted? Which things are not being counted?" They then have to pair the item they are counting with the correct number name. And finally, children must understand that the last number they say represents the number of objects they have counted (cardinality).

Even though young children like Darnella demonstrate their procedural knowledge of number through repeating the number sequence, they generally do not have an understanding of quantity. In order to accurately find quantity, children must have an understanding of one-to-one correspondence and cardinality. These important concepts develop during the prekindergarten years. Before then, children cannot accurately tag objects they are counting with the numbers that represent each object. It doesn't seem to bother them that there are 8 buttons and they've counted 10 (Copley, 2000).

When 2- or 3-year-old children are given seven chips and asked to count the chips, they might say, "One, two, three, four, five, six, seven, eight, nine, ten." Having memorized the order and names of the numerals, very young children can recite the numbers, but often count some of the chips more than once, or miss counting other chips. These children do not have an awareness of the fact that they are pairing the term *one* with the first object they are counting, the term *two* with the second, and so on. They should be able to accurately count smaller sets of objects, of less than five.

Counting to find quantity becomes more solidified for 4-year-olds. An example of understanding cardinality is shown by a child who says, "I'm not five yet. I'm this many," and counts four fingers, saying, "One, two, three, four! I'm four. Then I'll be five. It's this many," and holds up five fingers. Or, a child who counts the buttons on her coat. "One, two, three, four, five," she says. "I have five buttons on my coat." When children count rationally, they have constructed a mental structure of number and have assimilated number words into this structure. Now counting has become a rational tool for children to use when counting and solving problems.

Because counting, which is a part of children's everyday math knowledge, is essential to all other number operations, teachers deliberately foster counting in the early childhood curriculum. They do so by providing opportunities for children to learn the names of the numerals. More importantly, however, teachers structure the environment and curriculum in ways that put children face-to-face with problems that call for them to construct their own knowledge of number.

◇ **Key Concepts**

• Counting involves memorizing the names of the numerals.

• Counting to find quantity involves the understanding of one-to-one correspondence.

• Counting involves cardinality: understanding that the last number word said when counting a group of objects, such as *two,* represents two things, objects, events, and so on.

- Counting involves saying number words in a consistent, reproducible order.

- Counting involves abstraction—any thing can be collected and put in a group for counting.

- Counting involves the understanding that things can be counted in any sequence without changing the result.

- Counting leads to experiencing the number operations of adding and taking away and comparing quantities.

◇ Goals and Objectives

Research shows there are great variations in children's abilities to count (NRC, 2009). Early childhood educators will consider these individual differences as they select goals for children's counting experiences, as follows:

- Children will develop the disposition to count and use numbers in their everyday activities and experiences.

- Children will be able to count sequentially, eventually memorizing the sequence from 1 to 20, and then the patterns from 20 and beyond.

- Children will learn the names of numerals, and 4- to 5-year-olds will begin to write them.

- Children will have meaningful experiences counting to find out the quantity of items.

- Children will have meaningful opportunities to count to solve problems.

- Children will begin to use number operations in their everyday experiences.

◇ What You'll Need

The following books can enhance your knowledge and understanding of children's developing ability to count and how to best foster children's procedural and conceptual knowledge of number and counting.

Clements, D. H., & Sarama, J. (2009). *Learning and Teaching Early Math: The Learning Trajectories Approach.*

Copley, J. V. (2000). *The Young Child and Mathematics.*

National Research Council. (2001). *Adding It Up: Helping Children Learn Mathematics.*

Stenmark, J. K., Thompson, V., & Cossey, R. (1986). *Family Math.*

Children's Books

Because there are so many children's books that encourage counting, it is important to be discerning. The following meet the criteria for good children's literature as well as introducing children to number and counting.

Anno, M. (1999). *Anno's Magic Seeds.*

Anno, M. (1986). *Anno's Counting Book.*

Baker, K. (2004). *Quack and Count.*

Bang, M. (1991). *Ten, Nine, Eight.*

Base, G. (2006). *Uno's Garden.* For older children, this beautiful book is good for addition, subtraction, multiplication, and an emphasis on balance in the environment. The teacher can construct many investigations and games with this book as a basis.

Clements, A. (2006). *A Million Dots.*

Crews, D. (1968). *Ten Black Dots.*

Falwell, C. (2008). *Feast for 10.*

Gerth, M. (2001). *Ten Little Ladybugs.*

Grossman, V. (1998). *Ten Little Rabbits.*

Keats, E. J. (1999). *Over in the Meadow.*

Sayre, A. P., & Sayre, J. (2004). *One Is a Snail, Ten Is a Crab: A Counting by Feet Book.*

Viorst, J. (1988). *Alexander, Who used to Be Rich Last Sunday.*

Wood, J. (1992). *Moo, Moo, Brown Cow.*

Other Things You'll Need

- Materials that can be easily counted, such as counting chips, cubes, links, or pegs

- A math table complete set up with sorting bowls or cups, a balance scale, and a variety of materials for children to sort and count

- Plastic, magnetic, wooden, flannel-board, or other numbers for children to handle and sort

- Games that use dice or number cards, such as Candy Land, bingo, Sorry!, or Uno

- Materials that show numerals used for a purpose, such as calculators, calendars, receipt books, cell phones, menus or store circulars, and cash registers in the housekeeping area

- Environmental print that incorporates numbers

- A deck of cards

- Wooden beads

- Unifix cubes

 ## The Home–School Connection

Children can learn to count anywhere—at home, playing at the park, at the supermarket, in the child-care center—actually everywhere children are. Thus, building the home–school connection enhances children's opportunities to count and learn to use numbers with meaning. Remind parents that they can foster children's counting:

- Send home copies of counting poems and songs children sing or chant at school, so parents can sing or chant them with their children.

- Include counting books in the lending library for children to take home to "read" with their parents.

- Send home newsletters about how children learn to count through everyday experiences such as setting a table, cooking, or writing a shopping list. Sample newsletters are on the tear-out sheets on pages 76–79 at the end of this chapter.

- Invite parents to a workshop on mathematical learning for children. Explain to families how difficult it is for young children to learn all there is to know about counting. Encourage them to think just about the number "1" and all the things it could mean. For example, "My sister is 1 year old," "I can have one carrot," "I'm first," 1 minute, 1 hour, 1 day, or (as one child said during a discussion of the number), "I *won* the race!" Stopping to think carefully about something adults take so much for granted will encourage family members to be more interested in finding out what their children really know about numbers.

- At the end of the workshop, give parents copies of *More Than 1, 2, 3—The Real Basics in Mathematics,* written by Janet McCracken and published by the National Association for the Education of Young Children. These are $10 for 100 copies.

◇ Documenting and Assessing Children's Learning

Just as children naturally count throughout their day, teachers naturally evaluate and assess children's knowledge and understanding of counting. They observe children using numbers, question them, and challenge children by presenting problems and observing how they solve them.

Because each child will construct his or her own knowledge of counting, individual evaluation of children's counting abilities is called for. Work with individual children in the following ways:

- Following Ginsburg's (2009) assessment protocol, begin with observation, plan specific tasks to find out more information, and follow up with a flexible interview to learn more about children's thinking.

- *Observation.* Observe children as they play and document counting methods they engage in naturally. Reflect on observations and determine what you want to know more about, which should guide planning for specific tasks.

- *Task.* There are many different small, engaging tasks you could choose to use with children, depending on what it is specifically that you want to know. For example, using a Piagetian task, place a number of chips on a table in an irregular pattern and ask children to tell you how many chips there are, and then ask them to place the same number of chips on the table. Children just beginning to construct knowledge of number will likely place chips on the table, but not the correct number. At the next level, children will make a rough copy of the way the chips are arranged on the table. Then they will methodically look at the model and copy it, using fingers to point at the corresponding elements each time. When they have achieved concepts of number, they will count the number in the model and count the same number of chips.

- *Flexible interview.* After children complete a task, if you are interested in finding out more about what they know, you can follow up with some questions, such as "How did you know?" or "What did you do to figure it out?" You can also add additional tasks and questions, in order to challenge their thinking or to find out if they are able to do more with some support.

──────────────── **FOR THE CHILDREN** ────────────────

◇ **Learning About Numbers and Counting**

1. Children Will Develop the Disposition to Count and Use Mathematical Concepts in Their Everyday Lives

◆ In order for math learning to be beneficial to children in the long run, they have to learn to apply it to situations that require it. Not only is learning concepts and facts outside of real application no fun, but it doesn't teach children how math is used in the real world. Children's natural curiosity and openness to explore a wide variety of mathematical ideas should be fostered within the context of their real world (NCTM, 1989).

    The role of the early childhood educator is to foster children's natural inclination to count, to promote each child's success with numbers, and to provide children with meaningful firsthand experiences with numbers.

- Have board games available that involve counting, such as Candy Land and others. Make up card games; play Go Fish and other games that support number recognition, such as number bingo or Uno.

- Set up activities for children that encourage them to count. For example, using a muffin tin, place cutouts of different attribute shapes in the bottoms of each cup (cut out of the correct color of construction paper if possible). Label each shape with a different number of dots (1–6). Place the basket of attribute shapes next to the muffin tin. Children can take turns rolling a die, finding the number on one of the shapes, and then counting out the right number of shapes into the muffin cup.

- Provide children with a variety of manipulatives for counting and sorting. In clear plastic containers, you could supply the following:

  - Seashells, leaves, acorns, pine cones, rocks, jewels (sparkling stones)

  - Buttons that come in different sizes and colors and with different numbers of holes

  - Large marbles of different colors and types

  - Nuts, bolts, and screws

  - Pieces of plastic pipes and joiners

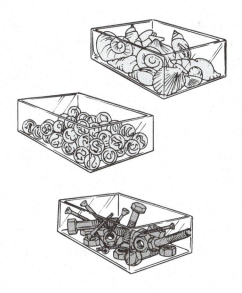

- Plastic or wooden animals, dinosaurs, birds, zoo animals, farm animals, trains, cars, or trucks to play with, count, and sort

- Ask parents to donate old keys to add to a counting collection

- Balancing scales. When placed near materials that are interesting to weigh, such as cotton balls, marbles, and counting cubes, children may want to count the items on each side to compare and contrast quantity versus weight.

◆ Opportunities for learning mathematics and counting should be positive and supportive. "Children must learn to trust their own abilities to make sense of mathematics" (NCTM, 2000, p. 2). Teachers of young children can support children's developing counting skills in the following ways:

- Provide children with different types of blocks—unit, parquet, and hollow—and the time and freedom to build and play with these in their own way. As children play, teachers observe and find ways to extend, expand, and build on children's existing knowledge of mathematics and counting. For instance:

- Count the number of unit blocks in a child's roadway.

- Ask if a child can build two structures that are the same height but using different sized blocks. Then count the blocks to compare.

- Very young children can explore one-to-one correspondence by putting one animal or one car on each block in a line.

- Ask children how many blocks they think they will need to fill in a certain space.

- During cleanup time, children can count the number of blocks they each put away.

- Use counting as a part of daily routines. One teacher occasionally used counting bears to take attendance in the morning. When each child arrived at school, they would place a bear in the balance scale—boys would place green bears on one side, and girls placed yellow on the other. During morning circle, the children looked at the balance scale to determine if there were more boys or more girls present. They then counted and compared groups to check.

- Add counting materials to the dramatic play area or areas. For example, add pretend coins and bills to wallets and purses to foster children's counting while shopping. Or, you could add these items:

  - Cellular or other phones to dial

  - Handheld calculators that work

  - Restaurant menus or grocery store circulars

  - Register receipts

  - Receipt books to fill in

  - Cash registers

  - Measuring cups and spoons

  - Tape measures, hourglasses, and other measuring tools

  - Old clocks and watches

  - Encourage children to use counting and numbers for specific purposes. When counting and numbers are necessary, children have a meaningful way to practice counting and to use numbers. For example:

    - When cooking, ask them to count the number of teaspoons, tablespoons, or cups required to make pudding, bread, or other foods using one-cup cooking. Barbara Johnson-Foote (2001) has developed cooking experiences in which each child follows a recipe for making just one portion of gingerbread, lemonade, and other healthful foods. In doing so, each child is following the pictures and printed recipe, measuring individual portions of food, to make his or her own serving.

- To find out information about the class or other topics of interest, ask children to consider other counting problems:

  - How many children are wearing something red or something blue?

  - How many children are wearing red shoes, blue shoes, new shoes, Velcro shoes, or tie shoes?

  - How many children have a cat for a pet, a dog, a fish, or no pet at all?

  - How many children like a particular color, poem, story, movie, or food?

  - How many children have baby brothers or sisters, how many have older brothers and sisters, and how many have no brothers or sisters?

  - How many birds come to the feeder in a given amount of time?

  - How many steps does it take to get to the playground?

- Help children to represent these findings in a graph, which they can use to interpret the data. This is a particularly important tool for early elementary students. In the early years, it is important for children to compare quantities to determine which has more or less. Graphs or charts are easy, visual ways for children to compare quantities.

◆ Not everything children count has to be concrete. For example:

  - How many days until someone's birthday? To make the task more concrete, make a paper chain with the number of days children have to wait for a birthday, a field trip, a party, or other special event. Each day, have a child take off one of

Children use numbers and charts to collect and reflect on information about class preferences.

the paper rings. The number remaining is the same as the number of days children have to wait for the event.

- How old is a child on his or her birthday? They could count fingers, chips, blocks, candles, and so on to make the task concrete.

2. Children Will Learn to Count Sequentially

◆ Counting rhymes and songs are a fun way to help young children learn the counting sequence.

For some counting rhymes, children can pretend to be the characters. For instance, when you chant "Five Little Speckled Frogs," invite one child to be a frog. To avoid conflict, designate a "pool" ahead of time: "When it's your turn to jump into the pool, where will you jump?" Children may choose a place on the floor, or decide to jump back to where they were sitting.

The first child will select enough children, counting herself, to make five frogs. Children mimic eating the lunch, then jump into the "pool" when the chant tells them to. When that group is finished, ask another child to start the game again until all who want to play have a turn at being a frog.

It is important for children to do the choosing. It gives them the opportunity to count themselves and figure out how many more children they need to make five frogs. If working with 5-year-olds, extend the number of frogs to 10. Do the same for other counting rhymes:

"Five (or Ten) Little Chickadees"

"Five (or Ten) Little Pumpkins"

"Ten in a Bed"

"Five Crocodiles"

"Five Little Monkeys"

◆   Using physical motions while counting helps children think more about the numbers they are saying. Children can choose a motion to use for each set of 10. For example, clap for each number 1 to 10, then stomp feet for 10 to 20, and so on. Older children may enjoy counting backward from 20, which can be done as a warning that it's almost time for cleanup, or one by one as children come back inside from outdoor play.

3. Children Will Learn the Names of the Numerals and How to Write Them

Because of the structure of the English language, children in the United States learn number names up to the number 20 by memorization. Once past 20, children need to understand the base-10 system and learn the repetition of the number pattern. Children often skip numbers later in the sequence or say them out of order, but the more they hear and say the correct sequence, the more accurate they will become (NRC, 2009).

Even though learning the conventional names of numbers involves rote memory, applying the number names to objects in order to quantify takes a lot of practice and additional understanding about number concepts. Further, the more embedded children's learning is in meaningful experiences, the greater the conceptual learning.

◆   Use children's literature to enhance children's knowledge of the names of numerals. There are so many counting books available that the teacher must use standards for good literature to judge them. *Ten Little Ladybugs* (Gerth, 2001), *Anno's Magic Seeds* (Anno, 1999), *Ten Little Rabbits* (Grossman, 1999), and *Fish Eyes: A Book You Can Count On* (Ehlert, 2001) are examples of excellent counting books. To use the books effectively for younger children, teachers should follow these guidelines:

  • Hold individual children on your lap and read a counting book together. Point to the numerals as you name them. Three-year-olds will enjoy listening over and over again to Jack Wood's *Moo, Moo, Brown Cow* (1992).

  • Obtain big books to read to the entire class, using a pointer or running your hands under the words and numerals as you read.

  • Use flannel, Velcro, or magnetic numerals and hold them up as they appear in a story. Place them on a board or hand them out to the children, who will hold them up when they appear again in the story or when you reread the story.

◆   Follow up story reading with a related activity. For example, after reading *Feast for 10* (Falwell, 2008), you could ask children about how many people sit at the

Teachers use different ways to represent numbers for children as they read counting stories.

table with them during dinner. Children can use pictures to represent the family members who eat dinner together and can create a class graph together showing the different numbers of family members.

After reading *Anno's Magic Seeds* (Anno, 1999), children could plant their own seeds. Label the plots with children's names. Keep track of how many days it takes for each seed to sprout, use measurement tools to document how tall each sprout grows, and document how many days it takes for blossoms and then fruit or vegetables to grow. Scarlet runner beans are good to plant because they sprout and grow rapidly, helping to hold young children's attention.

Read Ezra Jack Keats's *Over in the Meadow* (1990) several times so children become familiar with the rhythm and repetitive pattern of the book. Encourage children to notice the growing number pattern—that each page has *one more* animal than the last. At the end of the story, ask children to compare the numbers of things—for example, which animals were there more or less of than other animals?

◆ Make your own number book stories. Reading Donald Crews's (1985) *Ten Black Dots* may inspire children to be creative with numbers. Make books of newsprint pages with construction paper covers, as follows:

- Give 3-year-olds a book of three to five newsprint pages. Provide number stamps, number stickers, or number sponges for children to use in their books. Or ask children to count a small number of collage materials to glue on one page, count them together, and then write the number for them.

- Four-year-olds can be given books with more pages and choose to use stickers, print with rubber stamps, use other collage materials, or draw pictures of different numbers of objects. Four- and five-year-olds can also choose to attempt to write their numerals.

Remember that the objects children choose to print, stick, or draw on their pages do not have to be all the same. A set can consist of different objects. For example, a child could illustrate the page with the numeral 3 by choosing to place stickers of a car, a duck, and a flower on the page.

◆ Label plastic or paper bags with different numerals from 0 to 10. In a large or small group or during independent play, children can pick a bag and fill it with the correct number of objects. If working in pairs, children can exchange bags to check if their partner counted correctly.

◆ Play the "Freeze" game (optional music by Greg and Steve, *Kids in Motion*). For this game, the children listen to the music, and when it stops they have to freeze. One variation of the game is for the teacher to hold up a numeral or board with number pips on it while the children dance. When it's time to freeze, children hold up the correct number of fingers to match what the teacher is holding.

◆ Playing card games such as Uno encourages children to recognize numerals. Older children can play a version of War with smaller sets of cards, limited to the numbers 1–5 at first. In this game, children play in pairs and each put down one card. The child who puts down the larger number (or smaller, depending on the rules) gets to take both cards and puts them at the bottom of his or her pile. This continues until one child runs out of cards.

◆ Provide children with many opportunities to write numerals as well as letters:

   • In the writing center, include plastic numerals as well as letters. Also have a set of rubber or plastic-stamp numerals, sets of other plastic or rubber stamps, number stencils, and markers and papers for children to use to practice printing or writing numerals.

   • Provide calendars that have space for writing. Put these in the writing center or housekeeping area along with markers. You need not provide any directions—children will use them in different ways. Most, however, will begin copying the numeral in the space, giving them needed practice in writing numerals.

   • Place a number of small chalkboards and chalk on a table, or dry-erase boards and markers. Provide number cards or number magnets for children to use as models. Children will draw, scribble, and write on the boards depending on their age and developmental level—but with the numerals as a prompt, they will incorporate numerals in their writing.

   • In the art area, provide play-dough molds or presses that represent numerals. Provide sponges for paint that come in numerals, or small foam numerals for creating collages.

- In the writing center, children could choose how they want to make numerals. They could pick plastic or wooden numerals from a box and name them, print the numerals with rubber printing stamps, use a computer to print numerals, or use paper and markers to write them.

4. Children Will Have Meaningful Opportunities to Count Using One-to-One Correspondence

In order to count accurately, children need to understand the concept of one-to-one correspondence. For very young children, who are still not accurate at counting sets of objects, practice with matching up sets in a one-to-one way will prepare them for the future concept of matching up number names with sets of objects. Older children, who are already counting sets, do not need to learn one-to-one correspondence but still need practice with accurately tagging each object once and only once. Provide many different opportunities for children to count sets for a purpose.

◆ Everyday activities offer situations for matching one object or item to another:

- During snacks and lunchtimes, give children the opportunity to place one napkin, one fork, one spoon, and one glass at each place.

- Play musical chairs with enough chairs for all the children. Make the point that there is a chair for each child when the music stops.

Matching sets helps young children develop an understanding of one-to-one correspondence.

- During music time, have children clap their hands once to each beat of a drum, clap once for each syllable in their name, or clap when they sing or hear rhyming words.

- Construct matching games for children to play with and manipulate. A great matching game for younger children is one that has a mommy animal on one card and a baby animal on another. Creating pairs by matching is a precounting skill for very young children.

- In the block area, encourage children to create matching rows of blocks or to line up animals or cars, with just one on each block. Older children can count parking spaces to see if they have enough for each car or to figure out if there are enough train cars for each animal to sit on one.

- Play with parquet blocks. Place a row of blocks in front of a child and ask him or her to give each block a friend.

- Play "memory" games. Use commercial sets or make your own. Use number cards or picture cards. Children find pairs and match them together. After all pairs are found, older children can practice counting by 2s to see how many cards they have.

5. Children Will Begin to Use Number Operations in Connection with Their Daily Activities

Preschool children have been observed using a variety of strategies that involve number operations. By at least 3 years of age, most are able to use counting to perform simple addition and subtraction involving a few items, such as two blocks plus two blocks makes four blocks (NRC, 2009). Older preschoolers become much more adept at using numbers to solve problems and can do so with small sets (fewer than eight).

The role of teachers, then, is to observe children as they work with numbers and try to understand what children are thinking. To better understand their thinking, you might ask children how they found the right number of items or why they did what they did. Then, based on children's existing knowledge, teachers plan new experiences that clarify, expand, or extend that existing knowledge. Asking, "How did you know?" will provide you with information about what children understand as well as their errors in thinking.

◆ Everyday problems need number operations to be solved. You might try the following:

- Ask a child to count the number of chairs that need to be added to a group of chairs so each child has a place to sit. Or, have children count the number of chairs that need to be removed to match the size of the group.

- Involve children in using addition or subtraction in connection with their routines. For example, choose one child to pick enough children to make six, to take their turn brushing their teeth or getting their coats from the cubbies. Ask the children how many would have to wait if there were only room for four children.

◆ Use games that involve taking away and adding. Suggest a game to be played and demonstrate the game with a small group of children, or let children select a game from the counting table or math area (Seefeldt & Barbour, 1998). Playing the following games involves individual children or groups in counting, developing their disposition to use numbers and counting:

- **Mystery Box**

  Prepare a number of boxes by cutting a hole in one side of each box and placing a given number of small objects in each box. The child reaches into a box, feels the objects, counts them, and tells how many objects are in the box. Take the objects out of the box and count them again. Begin by placing two or three objects in a box and increase the numbers of objects as children gain counting skills.

- **Bowling**

  The child rolls a ball to knock down a group of objects—empty (cleaned) milk cartons, empty squirt bottles, or juice cans. After children roll the ball, they count the number of objects they have knocked down and how many are left and begin again. The goal is to knock all of the objects down. The game can be played alone, with a friend or two, or with the teacher, who will record children's knowledge of counting. Start with 5 and move up to 10.

- **Ring Toss**

  Using a hula hoop or a circle designated on the carpet with tape, have children work in pairs to toss small objects one at a time into the circle. Start with a set of five objects. The goal is not to get all five in the circle, but to document how many landed inside the circle and how many landed outside. Children can record their results on paper or dry-erase boards to share with each other as a class when they are done. This will demonstrate for children the different numbers that make up five (e.g., five inside and zero outside, or four inside and one outside).

- **Collections**

  You'll need boxes and collections of objects that fit in the boxes. Empty boxes are labeled "0," "1," "2," "3," and so on. Each child selects the specified number of objects from those provided to match the numeral on a box and puts them in the box. When this is done in groups inside, the boxes can be switched after each counting time. If the game is taken outside, the "zero" box can be left inside, or that can be the teacher box. Children can fill the boxes with found objects, rocks, stones, pine cones, or leaves. The idea is to count, so the objects in the box, or set, do not have to be all alike.

- **Dominoes**

  Demonstrate to a child or a small group of children how to play dominoes, matching a domino with four spots with another that has an equal number of spots. Encourage children to just find matching pieces.

- **Calendar Bingo**

  Mount pages from old or unused calendars on heavy cardboard. Identical mounted calendar pages are cut into individual number cards. The children match the individual numerals by placing them on the corresponding numerals on the uncut calendar.

- **Button, Button**

  Working with one child or a small group of children, give each child a handful of buttons of the same size, color, and shape. Allow children time to play with the buttons, trade them, match them, or make patterns with them, and then give children directions to follow: "Move two buttons to the middle of the table," "Put three buttons on top of one another," "Give four buttons to the person next to you." The number of buttons, and what children are to do with them, increases in difficulty as children mature and gain number concepts.

◇ **Reflecting**

Children can reflect on their counting experiences by organizing, presenting, applying, and communicating their knowledge of number and counting.

- Encourage children to document counting experiences in their math journals or number books.

- Structure opportunities for children to apply numbers for a purpose during the day. Ask them to count the number of children, apples, markers, or other objects needed. Ask them how many they have and how many more items they will need.

- From time to time, ask children to demonstrate their counting skills to others. During games or activities requiring counting, have children work in pairs to check each other's counting.

◇ **Extending and Expanding to the Primary Grades**

For Grade 1

Curriculum focal points and connections for grade 1 include (1) *Number and Operations* and *Algebra:* Developing understandings of addition and subtraction and strategies for basic addition facts and related subtraction facts, and (2) *Number and Operations:* Developing an understanding of whole number relationships, including grouping in 10s and 1s. The following content expectations are linked to the grade 1 focal points or connections:

- Develop an understanding of the relative position and magnitude of whole numbers and of ordinal and cardinal numbers and their connections.

- Develop a sense of whole numbers and represent and use them in flexible ways, including relating, composing, and decomposing numbers.

- Connect number words and numerals to the quantities they represent, using various physical models and representations.

- Understand various meanings of addition and subtraction of whole numbers and the relationships between the two operations.

- Understand the effects of adding and subtracting whole numbers.

  Some concrete experiences to reinforce the list just given include the following:

- Use interesting number stories to stimulate interest in creating counting books. Five-year-olds or older children can make fold-over booklets. Fold a piece of 12″ × 18″ construction paper in half and then in thirds. Cut between the folds to make doors. On the cover children print the numeral, and inside they draw a picture of one object, two objects, three objects, and so on. Children over age 6 can write a story as well. These books may be taken home to be read to younger siblings or donated to the preschool class in the building or neighborhood.

- Create a mural depicting a chant for 5- to 6-year-olds. For instance, if children love *Ten Little Rabbits,* you could take a long strip of mural paper and vertically mark spaces for the 10 numerals. Children working in small groups or individual children can volunteer to illustrate the numerals, drawing or painting the required number of rabbits for each space. Have children choose which numeral they will work on so each child gets a turn and no child has to draw 10 rabbits by him- or herself. For older children, make a more complex chart involving larger numbers of objects. If you use Velcro or tape for the objects and numbers, you can pose problems such as "What would happen if you moved two balls from line 11 to line 3?"

- Write a sequence of numbers and have children pick the number that comes next. Or create a sequence of numbers where certain numbers are missing. For older children, this can be done with number patterns of 2s or 5s.

- When children want to count aloud from 1 to 100, have them emphasize the patterns as they go. Have children stop at the "nine" and pause to prepare for the next set of 10s (e.g., "28, 29 . . . 30!"). This transition between sets is difficult, and giving a pause allows children to think about what comes next. Model the support of counting up by 10s to figure out what the next decade in the sequence is (e.g., "20 . . .30 . . .40. . . ?"). When children learn that this is a reliable method for helping them over the bump, they can think to themselves in the pause and get ready to start with the next decade. It is important that children sense the standard sequences of numbers before going on to other operations.

- Using children's collections, have them compare quantities using words such as *equal, less, fewer,* or *more.* Have them use counting to check their estimates. The number of objects in the collections may be larger as children grasp the concept.

- Read *Quack and Count* by Keith Baker. This attractive book introduces addition by dividing the seven ducks into different groupings. Using the book as a base, give children lots of manipulatives and play addition and subtraction games with the children. For example, "Danny has eight cubes. How many are left when two fall off of the table?" Give children lots of practice putting together and taking apart numbers.

For Grade 2

Curriculum focal points for grade 2 include (1) *Number and Operations:* Developing an understanding of the base-10 numeration system and place-value concepts, and (2) *Number and Operations* and *Algebra:* Developing quick recall of addition facts and related subtraction facts and fluency with multidigit addition and subtraction. The following content expectations are linked to the grade 2 focal points or connections for number and operations:

- Use multiple models to develop initial understandings of place value and the base-10 number system.

- Develop a sense of whole numbers and represent and use them in flexible ways, including relating, composing, and decomposing numbers.

- Understand situations that entail multiplication and division, such as equal groups of objects and sharing equally.

- Develop and use strategies for whole-number computations, with a focus on addition and subtraction.

- Develop fluency with basic number combinations for addition and subtraction.

- Use a variety of methods and tools to compute, including objects, mental computation, estimation, paper and pencil, and calculators.

For Grade 3

Curriculum focal points and connections for grade 3 include (1) *Number and Operations* and *Algebra:* Developing an understanding of multiplication and division and strategies for basic multiplication facts and related division facts, and (2) *Number and Operations:* Developing an understanding of fractions and fraction equivalence. The following content expectations are linked to the grade 3 focal points or connections:

- Understand the place-value structure of the base-10 number system and be able to represent and compare whole numbers and decimals.

- Recognize equivalent representations for the same number and generate them by decomposing and composing numbers.

- Develop an understanding of fractions as parts of unit wholes, as parts of a collection, and as locations on number lines.

- Use models, benchmarks, and equivalent forms to judge the size of fractions.

- Understand various meanings of multiplication and division.

- Understand the effects of multiplying and dividing whole numbers.

- Identify and use relationships between operations—such as division as the inverse of multiplication—to solve problems.

- Understand and use properties of operations.

- Develop fluency with basic number combinations for multiplication and division and use these combinations to mentally compute related problems, such as 30×50.

- Develop fluency in adding, subtracting, multiplying, and dividing whole numbers.

- Develop and use strategies to estimate the results of whole-number computations and to judge the reasonableness of such results.

- Select appropriate methods and tools for computing with whole numbers from among mental computation, estimation, calculators, and paper and pencil according to the context and nature of the computation, and use the selected method or tool.

Grade 3 focal points and connections are built from concepts learned and reinforced in the earlier grades. Counting is a foundation for students' early work with numbers. They begin to solve addition and subtraction problems by counting concrete objects. During the early elementary school years, they develop the ability to deal with numbers mentally and to think about numbers without having a physical model. Teachers may provide active experiences in a problem-solving context for children in this age group. For instance:

- Introduce tools used in mathematics—the calculator and selected computer programs. Children may have used the calculator previously, but now it becomes a tool to understand place value. A good open-ended activity suggested by the NCTM (2002) is to have students begin at one number and add or subtract until they reach a target number. Because there are no limits to the strategies students might use, this provides an excellent opportunity for students to discuss strategies employed.

- Introduce children to the symbols used in mathematics, such as = , + , − , and ×. An excellent book to assist with this process is Graeme Base's *Uno's Garden*

When supported by teachers, children can use computer programs to learn more about numbers and operations.

(2006). As the forest moves from good to bad and back to a balance, the composition changes. Children are introduced to more complex addition, subtraction, and multiplication in the context of an interesting and important story. The operations are placed conveniently in the upper right with the objects next to them. Also introduced in the back is the concept of prime numbers.

- It is also a good idea to connect number and operations with other subject matter areas. Specifically, science is tied closely to mathematics, and many scientific activities require mathematical or numerical thinking. Charts and graphs can be used to document outcomes of experiments or to keep records of collected data.

- Children are introduced to fractions early on, but in the early elementary years they begin to grasp concepts of division. Children's books that ask the characters to divide food or objects to accommodate more people are a good start. Teachers can use attribute blocks to begin discussions of fractions. The six triangles make up one hexagon, and three triangles make up the trapezoid. Base-10 blocks are another good material for teaching beginning fractions, as children find the many ways to get to 10 and then how 10s can be used to create 100, and so on.

- Children are interested in money and thinking of ways to make and spend it. Read *Alexander, Who Used to Be Rich Last Sunday* (1988) by Judith Viorst. Alexander was given some money by his grandparents, but somehow he spent it all and had nothing left. Have children read the story and keep track of how much money Alexander gave each person and how much money he has left after each transaction. Have children make a list of all the ways they could earn money and compare it with their classmates' lists.

Let's Think About Numbers!
1 2 3 4 5 6 7 8 9 10

Dear Families,

By now, you probably hear your children counting at some point every day. That's because young children love numbers! And there are many ways we can help children learn more about numbers, why they are so important, and what they mean.

There are things you may already do that help children think about numbers, such as:

- Counting as you walk up or down the stairs,
- Counting to find out how many there are of something, or
- Singing songs or reading books that have numbers in them

It is important to remember that we want children to learn their numbers, but we also want them to understand that numbers stand for things, such as one's age, how many of something you have, what order things come in, etc. So we want children to learn their number words, but more importantly, we want them to understand that numbers have meaning!

Here are some ways you can get your child thinking about numbers and their meanings:

- Ask your child to get you a certain number of eggs, to count back from 10 as the microwave finishes cooking, or to count to twenty while stirring a mixture.
- Give children responsibilities that include numbers, such as picking up a certain number of toys, using a specific amount of time to get something done, or counting out the right number of fruits or veggies to put in the shopping cart at the grocery store.
- Encourage children to look for numbers as you walk or drive to school and talk about what the different numbers mean (for example, identifying a car by its license plate, telling us how fast to drive on the speed limit sign, or telling us the price of food on a grocery store sign).

Your children love numbers, so find as many ways as you can to share in this interest and to help them understand even more about numbers and what they mean.

Number Songs

Dear Families,

We have attached a copy of the finger-plays and counting songs we have been learning here at school. Your child will likely be very excited to teach you the hand motions along with the tune of each song. These songs encourage children to count forward and sometimes backward and to represent numbers using their fingers and hands. Sing these songs with your children throughout the day and enjoy having some fun with numbers.

Assessing Children's Math Skills—Number & Operations

What to observe

Children playing games that require counting or number recognition (e.g., moving a certain number or spaces or matching number cards)

Children working in the math or manipulative center, using number puzzles, easily countable materials, and manipulatives that encourage counting such as counting bears, links, and pegs and peg boards

Children in the art area, using materials that encourage counting or number recognition, such as collage materials, play dough, or number stamps

Play in the block area. Children often count the number of blocks they use to create a structure or to determine who has a taller or bigger structure

Activities—for individual or group assessment

Count sets of objects to solve problems

Use counting to determine more than/less than, to solve problems, or to play a game

Use story problems relevant to classroom activities to demonstrate more than/less than or simple addition/subtraction problems

Write numbers and encourage children to write numbers in relationship to classroom activities or children's interests

Ask children to help you solve problems using numbers or operations

Example follow-up questions

What do you know about this shape?

Tell me how you knew these shapes were the same/different from these shapes?

Are there other shapes the same/different?

Is there another way you could do the same thing?

How do you know that it's symmetrical/congruent?

Strategies

Uses finger to "tag" objects when counting

Lines up objects before counting

Moves objects away from group when counting

Compares quantities by looking at sets

Compares quantities by counting objects in each set

Uses manipulatives to count, represent quantity, or solve simple addition/subtraction problems

Uses fingers to count, represent quantity, or solve simple addition/subtraction problems

Uses numerals or numerical symbols or pictures to count, represent quantity, or solve simple addition/subtraction problems

**Individual Evaluation: Assessing Children's Math Skills—
Number & Operations**

Date:

Child:

Area of classroom or activity:

Activity used:

Observation notes

Follow-up questions and responses:

Quick summary—Child:
Can say numbers correctly from 1 to 10
Can say numbers correctly from 10 to 20
Can extend the counting pattern beyond 29
Understands that the next number in the counting sequence represents one more than the previous number
Identifies numerals from 1 to 10
Identifies numerals from 10 to 20
Connects numerals with quantity
Correctly applies counting sequence to determine quantity
Understands the last number said represents the total number of objects
Understands terms such as more than, less than, same as
Uses manipulatives to solve simple addition/subtraction problems (total less than 5)
Uses manipulatives to solve simple addition/subtraction problems (total less than 10)
Represents addition or subtraction problems by drawing pictures

Learning the Basic Concepts of Algebra

―――――――――――― **FOR THE TEACHER** ――――――――――――

◇ What You'll Need to Know

Teachers of young children sometimes find it difficult to convey math concepts to their students because they have not been adequately prepared to teach it and receive little to no support through professional development opportunities or mentoring (Barnett, Epstein, Friedman, Stevenson-Boyd, & Hustedt, 2009; Copley & Padron, 1999; Lobman, Ryan, & McLaughlin, 2005). Teachers also often report mixed emotions about their own mathematics experiences, with many of them remembering a love of math until they reached a certain grade level. When considering algebra as a potential topic of study, teachers may worry that it is not something they are prepared to do. But during the early years, children learn basic concepts of algebra through everyday problem solving. They are natural problem solvers who are curious about everything in their environment and ask questions that invite the investigation of answers.

According to Taylor-Cox (2003), when we map the early experiences needed for success in learning formal algebra, we find several interconnected concepts that are developmentally appropriate and very applicable to early childhood education. Perhaps it is helpful to view algebra as the sum of various activities that young children already do spontaneously, but will need lots of opportunities to try in many situations and with diverse strategies. Basic experiences with algebra involve the following:

- The skills of classifying, sorting, and ordering objects

- The understanding of patterns—such as color, shape, number, and texture, as well as those involving kinesthetic, tactile, visual, or auditory stimuli

- The use of concrete and pictorial representations that will later develop into symbolic notations

- Addition and subtraction

- The understanding of quantitative changes in things, such as plants growing larger

- The understanding of qualitative changes in things, such as recognizing that one tree is larger than the one next to it

Curriculum focal points (NCTM, 2006) recommended for content emphasis in prekindergarten and kindergarten are discussed in the following paragraphs, as are the related expectations for prekindergarten and kindergarten considered essential for learning basic concepts of algebra. Expectations through grade 3 are highlighted at the end of the chapter in the section titled "Extending and Expanding to the Primary Grades."

Algebra is not considered a curriculum focal point for prekindergarten. Rather, it is seen as connecting to number and operations, geometry, and measurement. Through learnings in these areas, children recognize and duplicate simple sequential patterns (for example: square, circle, square, circle, square, circle). Related expectations for algebra include the following:

- Sorting, classifying, and ordering objects by size, number, and other properties

- Recognizing, describing, and extending patterns, such as sequences of sounds and shapes or growing numeric patterns

- Analyzing how both repeating and growing patterns are generated

- Describing qualitative change, such as a student growing taller

As with prekindergarten, kindergarten curriculum focal points are seen as connecting to the three curriculum focal points mentioned earlier. Children identify, duplicate, and extend simple number patterns and sequential and growing patterns (for example, patterns made with shapes) as preparation for creating rules that describe relationships. The following content expectations are linked to the kindergarten focal points or connections:

• Sort, classify, and order objects by size, number, and other properties.

• Analyze how both repeating and growing patterns are generated.

• Use concrete, pictorial, and verbal representations to develop an understanding of invented and conventional symbolic notations.

• Describe qualitative change, such as a student growing taller.

The teacher will provide many experiences for young children that foster these skills. Some will come from children's everyday interactions with materials; others will be carefully planned to expose children to basic concepts. Gradually, through active experiences with the components of algebra, children will form the foundations on which later abstract learning can be built.

Copley (2000) suggests that there are questions specific to patterns, functions, and algebra. They are designed to facilitate children's thinking and sharpen their problem-solving skills. Examples include the following:

"Do you see a pattern? Tell me about it."

"I see that you organized your materials in a specific way. Can you tell me about it?"

"What comes next? Could we make the same pattern with these different materials?"

"How can we remember this pattern? Could we make a picture that will help us? Could we use numbers instead?"

"These Cuisenaire rods keep getting longer. Can you help me find the one that comes next?"

"Can you clap your pattern?"

◇ Key Concepts

• Patterns exist everywhere in a variety of shapes, sizes, colors, and numbers.

• It is possible to repeat and extend patterns as in music.

• Groups of various items may be sorted, classified, and ordered by one or more attributes.

• The addition and subtraction of whole numbers may be represented using objects, pictures, and symbols.

• Addition and subtraction sentences may be constructed. *More* suggests addition, and *less* suggests subtraction. *Equals* suggests that both sides of the sentence are equal or the same.

• A variety of things may change in quality and in quantity.

◇ Goals and Objectives

The following depend on children's age and grade:

- Children will identify patterns in a variety of ways—not only in numbers, but also in designs, music, and movement.
- Children will copy, create, and interpret patterns.
- Children will repeat and extend patterns.
- Children will describe quantitative and qualitative changes in living things. (This goal is best left for kindergarten or early elementary children.)
- Children will be introduced to symbols through concrete representations.
- Children will sort, classify, and order a variety of concrete objects by one or more attributes.
- Children will begin to use simple mathematical terminology.

◇ What You'll Need

The National Council of Teachers of Mathematics (NCTM; see References and Resources) has many fine publications and Web resources. One book that may be useful for understanding teaching and learning algebra in the early years is NCTM's *Algebra in the Early Grades* (2007). The book provides a concrete description of algebraic thinking, as well as best practices for introducing algebraic concepts into classroom activities. The joint position statement of NAEYC and NCTM (2002) suggests that algebraic thinking should receive somewhat less emphasis in the early childhood curriculum—with the exception of patterning, which merits special mention because it is accessible and interesting to young children, eventually undergirds all algebraic thinking, and supports the development of other conceptual areas. Young children are naturally inclined to organize and classify materials they encounter and can be helped to understand and reflect on what they are doing.

Keeping in mind that children construct their own knowledge through active experiences, the following books will help you to refresh your memory on algebra and to plan activities for the children you teach:

Greenes, C., Cavanagh, M., Dacey, L., Findell, C., & Small, M. (2001). *Navigating Through Algebra in Prekindergarten–Grade 2 (with CD-ROM)*. Demonstrates how some fundamental concepts of algebra can be introduced. The most helpful part for teachers of young children may be the section on repeating and growing patterns.

Hurst, C. O., & Otis, R. (1996). *Picturing Math*. Has an excellent chapter on patterns and picture books. Hurst and Otis include the developmental stages in introducing patterns, a few pattern activities for several age groups, and annotated picture books for patterns.

Kohl, M. A., & Gainer, C. (1997). *Math Arts: Exploring Math Through Art for 3 to 6 Year Olds*. Has many good ideas for using art to foster emergent math skills and concepts.

Payne, J. N. (Ed.). (1990). *Mathematics for the Young Child*. Designed for teacher educators and teachers of children in preschool through grade 4. It is full of activities; however, a close examination shows fewer for the younger grades. Some activities can be adapted for younger children.

Schiller, P., & Peterson, L. (1997). *Count on Math: Activities for Small Hands and Lively Minds.* An activity-oriented program for children ages 3 to 7.

Thiessen, D., Matthias, M., & Smith, J. (1998). *Wonderful World of Mathematics: A Critically Annotated List of Children's Books in Mathematics* (2nd ed.). A valuable collection of short reviews of children's books with mathematical content. Again, you may want to look closely for books for preschoolers. If you do, you will be rewarded with an excellent book to inspire an active mathematics experience.

Children's Books

Aardema, V. (1975). *Why Mosquitoes Buzz in People's Ears.*

Anno, M. (1987). *Anno's Math Games.*

Barton, B. (1991). *The Three Bears.*

Base, G. (2006). *Uno's Garden.*

Brown, M. W. (1947). *Goodnight Moon/Buenas Noches Luna.*

Carle, E. (1994). *The Very Hungry Caterpillar.*

Crews, D. (1968). *Ten Black Dots.*

Dee, R. (1988). *Two Ways to Count to Ten: A Liberian Folktale.*

De Regniers, B. S. (1985). *So Many Cats!*

Fox, M. (1990). *Shoes from Grandpa.*

Harris, T. (2000). *Pattern Fish.*

Hoban, T. (1986). *Shapes, Shapes, Shapes.*

Hoban, T. (1987). *Dots, Spots, Speckles, and Stripes.*

Holm, S. L. (2003). *Zoe's Hats: A Book of Colors and Patterns.*

Hopkins, L. B. (Ed.). (1997). *Marvelous Math: A Book of Poems.*

Hutchins, P. (1986). *The Doorbell Rang.*

Martin, B. (2008). *Brown Bear, Brown Bear, What Do You See?*

Martin, B., Jr., & Archambault, J. (1989). *Chicka Chicka Boom Boom.*

McKissack, P. C. (1997). *Mirandy and Brother Wind.*

McMillan, B. (1986). *Becca Backward, Becca Forward: A Book of Concept Pairs.*

Numeroff, L. J. (1985). *If You Give a Mouse a Cookie.*

Rathman, P. (2000). *Goodnight Gorilla.*

Ring, S. (2002). *I See Patterns.*

Reid, M. (1990). *The Button Box.*

Swinburne, S. R. (2002). *Lots and Lots of Zebra Stripes: Patterns in Nature.*

Tang, G. (2002). *Math for All Seasons.*

Other Things You'll Need

- Containers of all types for sorting—including egg cartons, muffin tins, fish bait boxes, different-sized and -colored bowls

- Doll and animal families that come in three or more sizes

- Objects of all kinds for sorting, classifying, and ordering

- Deck of cards or other games with number cards
- Cubes and pattern blocks
- Lacing beads and other materials to string
- Pegs and pegboards
- Matching card games such as *Memory*, *Uno*, or bingo
- Geoboards
- Parquetry blocks and patterns
- Colored tiles
- Balances and weights
- Music, songs, or finger-plays with different rhythms and pattern repetitions
- Paper, drawing tools, collage materials, pom-poms, and other art supplies
- Paint sample strips with different shades of colors
- Magazines and photographs featuring patterns on buildings, sidewalks, and so forth
- Materials from nature that come in different sizes, such as shells, pine cones, or pebbles

Some materials are developed specifically to encourage sorting and classifying. These counting bears come in different colors that children naturally want to organize and sort in various ways.

The Home–School Connection

There are many things that families can do to enhance emergent math skills and concepts in algebra. Once families are made aware of the importance of patterns in children's developing math skills, they will be more likely to find ways to explore them in their everyday environments. There are plenty of things in the home, yard, grocery store, and so on to provide curious children with active experiences in math. Sample newsletters for parents are on the tear-out sheets on pages 96 and 97.

The U.S. Department of Education has published a book for parents and their young children, *Early Childhood: Where Learning Begins—Mathematics: Mathematical Activities for Parents and Their 2- to 5-Year-Old Children* (Fromboluti, Rinck, Magarity, & Gibson, 1999). It may be obtained from the Department of Education or from the Web. It emphasizes problem-solving, communication, and questioning skills for both children and parents. The following daily activities are suggested for enhancing emergent skills in algebra. You can convey them to parents through a newsletter, a bulletin board, a conference, or an algebra party.

- As children get dressed, ask them to look for patterns in their clothing. Then ask them to tell you about the patterns.

- Discuss the events of the day with your children. This will help them to understand that a regular sequence of daily events can be another pattern.

- Setting the table at mealtime can reveal patterns. The knife, fork, plate pattern repeats as you move around the table.

- On the way to school, point out how the shapes of street signs help people know what each sign means. The link between symbols and the concepts they represent is key to algebra learning, but not clear to young children.

- When waiting in the doctor's office or other places, encourage children to look for patterns on the rug, wallpaper, ceiling tiles, or furniture.

- At the grocery store, foods are organized in a specific way and grouped together by attributes. Children can help you find foods by thinking about how they are like other foods. When you get home, children can sort the groceries by their

Children notice interesting patterns on each other's clothing

relationships, or the part of the store they come from. Or, they can sort them by where they belong in the kitchen or pantry. Allow children to make decisions about where things should go, using their understanding of shared attributes to build relationships.

- Any time the family laundry is being done is a chance for sorting and matching games. Children learn the concept of multiple ways to organize, sort, and re-sort. If there are patterns or colors on clothing, point them out as a clue for matching.

◇ Documenting and Assessing Children's Learning

In order for teachers to discover what children know and what skills they are still developing, they need to observe children as they play with materials that encourage algebraic thinking. Teachers may also design activities for children that are interesting to them and allow them to demonstrate their knowledge and abilities. Often the teacher will observe children to document what is of interest to them and suggest various questions that they might want to answer as part of an investigation. With the teacher's support, children can observe and document patterns and relationships that are interesting to them and share findings with the rest of the class. Discoveries may be documented through pictures, graphs, or other types of representation and used by teachers and children to reflect on ideas, reach some conclusions, ask new questions, and plan for new investigations.

Chapters 1, 9, and 10 have many examples of ways that teachers can document and assess children's learning. Charts of all kinds, diagrams, graphs, and other visual representations validate children's efforts and allow them to use solutions to previous problems to help guide them toward solutions for new problems.

Digital cameras assist teachers in documenting the work that the children have done. An inexpensive digital camera can be made available for children to use as a way to document their own work or things of interest. Teachers use children's portfolios to keep their drawings, stories, and other evidence of their understanding of basic concepts of algebra, and children are invited to submit work they are proud of to add to their portfolios.

Teachers can plan more effectively for classroom instruction when they are aware of their children's development and interests. By establishing a regular system of assessing and documenting children's work, teachers can use that information to plan activities and experiences either to challenge children who have mastered certain skills or to provide extra support for children who need additional help. Assessment is one part of the cycle of planning, teaching, and assessment and is done on an individual and group basis using methods like these:

- Observations

- Planned activities with small groups or individual children

- Structured interviews with students at intervals during the school year

- Children's math journals

- Portfolios of children's work

- Children's self-evaluations and dictated stories about math concepts

The tear-out assessment sheets on pages 98 and 99 at the end of this chapter can be used throughout the school year to document growth in children's thinking and to help you plan your curriculum on the basis of children's current understandings.

———————————— **FOR THE CHILDREN** ————————————

◇ **Learning Algebraic Concepts**

This section attempts to treat each of the components of early numeracy in algebra. First, among the earliest skills children develop are identifying attributes and organizing materials by their attributes. This is sorting or classifying. Then, once children understand classification, they begin to classify by specific rules, such as patterns. Although children may be able to identify patterns early on, creating patterns requires skills in classification. Children learn to identify specific relationships among objects and materials and order them in specific ways. Finally, ideas for the addition and subtraction of whole numbers using objects, pictures, and symbols will be presented. The teacher will recognize that each of the components is connected and understand that individual children will develop skills in these areas at different times. The teacher may want to encourage children to keep a math journal to record the concepts they have learned. For younger children, this might consist of simple labeled drawings, or an illustration of a basic concept such as the pattern on a leaf. Older children may make drawings of their investigations of objects and symbols, and teachers can take dictation of their explanations.

1. Children Will Learn to Identify Attributes and Sort Objects by Various Attributes

Young children begin the process of classification by identifying objects by attributes such as color, size, or function. Once they begin to notice similarities and differences among objects, they become interested in sorting them into groups. Many preschool math materials are designed to encourage children to sort or classify, such as different colored blocks or counting bears, pegs and peg boards, and counting cubes. Some materials even provide self-correcting supports, such as colored bowls that match the colors of the counting bears, allowing children to easily sort correctly. Seefeldt and Barbour (1998) suggest that before children can classify, they must have some concept of "belongingness," "put together," and "alike." Consequently, the role of the teacher is to provide children with many opportunities to identify materials by their attributes and encourage children to organize materials in different ways.

◆ Provide children with boxes of scrap materials—velvet squares, tweeds, and net—all cut into uniform sizes and shapes for feeling, sorting, and classifying according to texture. Once they have organized materials according to texture, ask children to use another attribute, such as color. Using other categories of things will keep the interest of the children alive. Try objects like these:

A box of keys

Greeting cards

A button box

Shells, seeds, leaves, and rocks found in the outdoor environment

A bin full of different bottle caps

Muffin tins or small baskets next to containers of pom-poms, lacing beads, links, and so on

Bolts, nails, screws—this adds the dimension of function

◆ Play matching games such as *Memory*, *Uno*, or bingo, which encourage children to pay attention to attributes and sort materials by 2s, into groups of matching sets.

◆ Play pattern *Simon Says*. Create patterns for children to copy with movements such as clapping, stomping, or hopping. Encourage children to create their own movement patterns for others to copy.

◆ During transitions, ask children to line up or go to the table by an attribute they do or do not have. For example, "If you are *not* wearing blue, you can go wash your hands," or, "If you do *not* have brown hair, go line up." For younger children, using an attribute they *do* have will be less challenging.

◆ Play "One of these things is not like the other." This game can vary in complexity depending on the ages of the children. Show them three or four objects, one of which is different from the others in an obvious or more subtle way. For example, for younger children, you might place three triangles and a square and ask them which one is different. Other attributes you could vary include color, function, gender (i.e., three boy dolls and a girl doll), and so on. Older children can participate by making their own sets and asking you or other children to guess.

◆ Provide children with art materials such as pom-poms or rainbow ice pop sticks, different-colored foam blocks or inch cubes, attribute blocks that vary by shape, size, and color, and so on. The older the children, the more ways they will find to order a set of objects. Remember that preschool children will have difficulty sorting objects by more than one attribute. Older children might enjoy the challenge of trying to sort by two attributes, such as small and large buttons with four holes and small and large buttons with two holes.

◆ Provide muffin tins or small baskets near containers of small sorting toys. Older children can create their own sorting rules. Younger children may be supported by placing different-colored circles or numbers on the bottom of each muffin hole to guide the sorting.

2. Children Will Discover Patterns and Relationships

According to Clements and Sarama (2009), the concept of "pattern" in preschool is often limited to the basic repetitive pattern of ABAB, but they view patterning as "the search for mathematical regularities and structures" (p. 190). If it is thought of as a process, rather than a specific content area, the exploration of patterns can take on whole new meaning. It is through the early exploration of sequential and repeated patterns that children begin to learn the process of patterning that will support future mathematical understanding.

From an early age, children are interested in patterns and observe and point them out in their environments. Patterns are experienced in a variety of ways—not only in physical repetitions, but also in numbers, in designs and arrangements, in music and finger-plays, and in recurring events, such as the daily schedule or the days of the week. Children use their understanding of patterns as a tool for solving problems and making predictions and eventually use it to better understand number patterns. Model identifying patterns and encourage children to find patterns inside and outside the classroom. The daily schedule, the way children sit around the table, the collage array on a child's artwork, or the blocks used to build a tower may all present unique patterns that will not be immediately obvious to children. Pointing out patterns that you see in the environment will help children to become more sensitive to the patterns they observe and create. Outside, identify patterns in nature and in the playground or neighborhood environment. See the box titled "Generalizations About Natural and Human-Made Patterns" on page 90.

Researchers suggest that there are developmental stages in the understanding of patterns. Most children enter preschool with the ability to identify simple patterns, and preschoolers can learn to copy such patterns. Older children may be able to create their own patterns or extend patterns created for them (Clements & Sarama, 2009; National Research Council [NRC], 2009). In kindergarten, students can create and extend more complex patterns. They are also able to generalize, creating a pattern similar to another one in its form, but differing in attribute. For example, after seeing a *blue*, *red*, *red*, *blue* pattern, they can create a *green*, *yellow*, *yellow*, *green* pattern. This ability is essential to using the structure of patterns to solve problems. By grades 1 and 2, the ability to recognize complex patterns increases and children get better at creating their own patterns. Later they can manipulate those patterns in a variety of ways.

GENERALIZATIONS ABOUT NATURAL AND HUMAN-MADE PATTERNS

- Patterns are made of parts.
- Patterns can be defined by specific characteristics.
- Patterns are repetitious.
- Patterns provide structure.
- Patterns can be used to predict outcomes.
- Patterns provide a framework for learning.
- Patterns can be simple or complex.
- Patterns can overlie one another.
- Patterns can be experienced through many different senses.
- Patterns can grow and change.

Start with simple activities for younger children and do not ask them for a "right" answer. Their experimentation and observation skills will lead them to mature conclusions as they progress.

◆ Read and chant any book that contains a regular patterned chorus, such as *Chicka Chicka Boom Boom*, *Brown Bear, Brown Bear, What Do You See?*, or *If You Give a Mouse a Cookie*. The pattern is in the rhythmic chant and in the repetition of words and/or events. Some books, such as *The Very Hungry Caterpillar*, *Goodnight Gorilla*, and *There Was an Old Lady Who Swallowed a Fly*, include growing patterns that children love to learn and repeat. These growing patterns are directly related to and will help children better understand concepts of seriation and number patterns.

◆ Read the book *I See Patterns*. For young children, patterns in the environment are not always immediately apparent. This book will help children understand the different types of patterns and where they exist in the environment. Returning to this book often will encourage children to explore their own environment and find patterns around them both inside and outdoors.

◆ With younger children, play "head, shoulders, knees, and toes" to become familiar with patterns. Later extend this pattern to "clap, shoulders, shoulders, knees; clap, shoulders, shoulders, knees." Ask children to create their own patterns with clapping or stomping or slapping their knees.

◆ Use art activities to encourage children's recognition and creation of patterns. Provide collage materials that come in different shapes and sizes, such as small foam shapes, cotton pom-poms that come in different sizes, rainbow-colored ice pop sticks, and individual hole punches that come in various shapes or designs. Model making patterns with materials as a suggestion for ways in which children can use materials, and identify patterns children make in their own artwork. Make sure to always use three complete units of the pattern before asking children to identify it.

◆ Children can create collages using tissue paper, scraps of cloth, and old magazines with interesting patterns. Have children describe the patterns they have created or the patterns they see in the materials. Cut up strips of paint samples from a hardware store so children can create new color patterns or seriated (growing) patterns.

◆ Use a linear calendar or daily schedule to help children identify the patterns that exist in time. Using "school days" and "home days" will show children the repetition of 5 days, then 2 days, and so on. With the daily schedule, children will begin to recognize the pattern of events and how they repeat each day.

◆ Use books of photographs and other children's books to illustrate patterns. *Goodnight Moon* by Margaret Wise Brown is full of patterns. Colors darken as night approaches, and toys change in size. The author has carefully based her book on the patterns of going to sleep. *Dots, Spots, Speckles, and Stripes* by Tana Hoban uses vivid photographs to illustrate patterns in feathers, flowers, people, and animals. Children may draw their own scene from the story, using patterns they observe in the book or creating their own.

◆ Use popular physical activities to illustrate the concept of pattern—for example, step, hop, hop, step, hop, hop; or hands up, hands down, hands out. Once the children have mastered a pattern, they will be able to predict the movement that comes next. Always ask them to describe the pattern. Older children may be able to explain it in symbols.

◆ Use music to illustrate the concept of pattern. Three good music CDs from Ella Jenkins are *Jambo and Other Call-and-Response Songs and Chants* (1996), *You'll Sing a Song and I'll Sing a Song* (1989), and *This Is Rhythm* (1994). These discs, available from Smithsonian Folkways Recordings, should assist children in building concepts of pattern through music. Encourage children to use musical instruments to repeat patterns they hear in music or to create their own musical patterns.

3. Children Will Use Knowledge of Patterns to Begin Exploring Number Concepts

As children become more familiar and more competent with patterns, they may begin to see similarities in number patterns. Older preschoolers may want to count by 2s or 10s, especially if they have older siblings who do so. They will also learn the number patterns that begin after the number 20. Early addition skills begin with a growing "plus 1" pattern, where children add 1 by counting up. Older children will be able to add 2 by counting up in sets of two numbers. Using manipulatives to solve addition problems also demonstrates for children that in addition, $2 + 3 = 3 + 2$. When the two sets are counted to find out the total, it makes no difference if you start with the set that has two or the set that has three; you will still arrive at the same answer. This early understanding is the beginning of the connection between patterns and algebraic thinking (Clements & Sarama, 2009).

◆ Read *Two Ways to Count to Ten: A Liberian Folktale* by Ruby Dee. The book illustrates two ways to count to 10—by 2s as well as 1s. Take various even numbers and see if the children can figure out ways to count to the end number. If the children are young, give them any number of manipulatives and see if they can sort them into equal groups that will add up to the original number given them. The folktale also illustrates the point that the winner is the one who thinks carefully about how he will solve the problem.

◆ Read *The Doorbell Rang* by Pat Hutchins. Ma bakes cookies for Sam and Victoria to share. But—the doorbell rings and each time it rings, more and more friends come to share the plate of cookies. This leaves fewer and fewer cookies for the children to divide until Grandma arrives with fresh cookies. Divide the class into pairs. Give each pair 20 identical objects and ask them to find various ways to put them into equal groups. Ask one child to record their findings. Then ask them to repeat the activity two more times, first using 18 objects and then using 12 objects. Reflect together as a whole class on the solutions found. Find similarities and differences among the different sets. For example, the sets of 12 and 18 could be evenly split into groups of 3, but the set of 20 could not. Ask children if they can find other numbers that can be divided evenly into 3s.

◇ **Reflecting**

Ask children to organize their experiences. Provide them with exhibit space so that they can display their Lego structures, lacing bead patterns, and artwork. Kindergartners may want to keep a pattern journal. This journal could be used to record patterns observed in the environment and to create new patterns with shapes, colors, or numbers.

Make a collaborative class pattern quilt. Invite families to participate by sending home art materials for families to create their own, unique pattern strip. Family members can create individual pattern strips or one that represents the whole family. Once children have brought their pattern strips back to class, work together to attach the patterns to a large mural paper or to a bulletin board, creating a new pattern out of the pattern strips. Engage the children by asking them to organize the strips in such a way that makes sense to them. Make sure the quilt is in an area where parents and family members can easily see it when they drop off or pick up their children each day.

◇ **Extending and Expanding to the Primary Grades**

For Grade 1 and Grade 2

Algebra alone is not considered a curriculum focal point for grade 1 or grade 2 (NCTM, 2006). It is connected to number and operations as children use beginning concepts of commutativity and associativity in simple addition and subtraction problems. They also explore and identify number patterns, such as odd and even, and use them to solve problems. Children in second grade begin to extend their understanding of number patterns, such as skip counting, and can use them to solve problems involving multiples. Additionally, growing patterns become more interesting and can be expanded to help children consider numbers, geometry, and measurement.

Related expectations for grade 1 and grade 2 include the following:

- Use concrete, pictorial, and verbal representations to develop an understanding of invented and conventional symbolic notations.

- Model situations that involve the addition and subtraction of whole numbers, using objects, pictures, and symbols.

- Describe quantitative change, such as a student's growing 2 inches in one year.

Word problems elicit older children's reasoning about basic algebra.

For Grade 3

Algebra is not considered a curriculum focal point for grade 3. It is connected to other focal points as children begin to understand properties of multiplication and division. The creation and analysis of patterns and relationships involving multiplication and division should occur at this grade level. Students build a foundation for later understanding of functional relationships by describing relationships in context with such statements as, "The number of legs is 4 times the number of chairs" (NCTM, 2006, "Curriculum Focal Points and Connections for Grade 3").

Related expectations for grade 3 include the following:

- Describe, extend, and make generalizations about geometric and numeric patterns.

- Represent and analyze patterns and functions, using words, tables, and graphs.

- Express mathematical relationships, using equations.

- Model problem situations with objects and use representations such as graphs, tables, and equations to draw conclusions.

Children in the early primary grades can do the following:

- Understand the concepts of repeating and growing patterns and articulate the principles behind them. The teacher may start by giving children the principle (add two cubes to each side) and then encourage them to experiment with different ideas.

- Understand more complex patterns and how they are used. A famous illustrator of children's picture books, Jerry Pinkney, uses quilts in each of his books. He believes they are the fiber that holds a culture together. (See *Mirandy and Brother Wind* by Patricia C. McKissack, illustrated by Jerry Pinkney.) The teacher may ask older children to discuss the concept of pattern in this or other contexts. How would we function without patterns? Read the poem "Math Makes Me Feel Safe" by Betsy Franco, in L. B. Hopkins's *Marvelous Math: A Book of Poems.*

- Utilize more abstract concepts in ordering or determining what is different in a pattern. *Anno's Math Games* by Mitsumasa Anno has many challenges for the young elementary school student in the area of emergent algebra skills. The games are also appropriate for other math content areas.

- Understand simple equations, especially in concrete form. For example, using balance scales and Unifix cubes, children can experiment with balancing sets of concrete objects. Teachers may extend this knowledge to exploring various ways of representing their equations conventionally. Of particular importance here is helping children understand the meaning of the equals sign, in that it represents equality between both sides of the equation. Representing addition and subtraction problems in various ways (e.g., $4 = 3 + 1$, or $5 + 3 = 2 + 6$) allows children to understand the equals sign correctly, rather than incorrectly thinking it means "the answer" or "what comes next."

- Understand that items can be classified in more than one way. Read *The Button Box* by Margarette Reid. In this book, a young boy explores his grandmother's box of buttons, grouping or classifying them according to various qualities. He imagines interesting stories behind the different buttons. Examples of classifications for the same group of buttons can be color, smallest to largest, and then largest to smallest (reversibility). Children at this age can classify objects by more than one attribute at a time. Ask children to work in pairs or small groups to sort buttons by a rule while the other children attempt to identify the rule.

- More easily describe qualitative and quantitative changes. Linking mathematics with science investigations may facilitate the acquisition of these concepts. Describing the changes in plants and seeds and using comparison words help children to understand change. Measuring and recording changes in height or weight in journals or on graphs helps with quantitative thinking and connects to concepts of data collection and interpretation.

- Ask better and more specific questions, make better predictions, and use multiple strategies to solve problems and more accurately represent problems and solutions and explain them to others (using the "mathematician's chair"—see Chapter 10).

- Design their own simple experiments and math games based on children's literature or ideas from the classroom or play yard.

- Utilize computers to explore online problems. Teachers will want to make sure ahead of time that the sites are suitable and simple to navigate. Some such sites include www.ezschool.com, www.pbs.org, and www.mathtoybox.com/patblocks3/patblocks3.html.

- Build a larger vocabulary of mathematical terms. These may be recorded in children's math journals, put on word walls, and posted in the math area of the classroom for easy reference.

- Read *Uno's Garden* by Graeme Base. In this charming environmental book, elementary students are introduced to the concept of balance using addition, subtraction, and multiplication as the forest is reduced to 0 animals, $0 \times 0 = 0$ plants, and $256 + 256$ buildings which equals $(=)$ 512 buildings. Slowly the process reverses so that there are $10 \times 10 = 100$ animals, $10 \times 10 = 100$ plants, and $10 \times 10 = 100$ homes. There are also number games embedded in the story.

• Read *Ten Black Dots*. Ask children to make their own dot books, using different numbers of dots to create new pictures. Before creating their books, though, children will need to determine how many dots each will need for their books. This problem can be worked on in groups, with solutions shared with the class. Once the correct answer is agreed on, some children may be interested in figuring out how many dots will be needed by the whole class for all children to make their own books. Encourage the use of counters, calculators, and other math materials to help children find a solution.

Making a Class Quilt

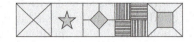

Dear Families,

We have been talking a lot about patterns in our classroom and exploring many different ways to make patterns. We wanted to ask you to help us make a class quilt of patterns.

Inside this kit you will find:

- Several long strips of construction paper
- Many different scraps of wrapping paper, cloth, and collage materials
- Glue sticks
- Markers

Directions:

- Together with your child and anyone else in the family who would like to participate, choose the materials you would like to use to create your patterns. Plan the pattern, and use the glue stick to glue the materials onto the strips of construction paper in the pattern of your choosing. Encourage your child to choose his own pattern, whether it be simple or more complicated.

- Talk about the different kinds of patterns you made and the ways they are similar and different. Did you choose the same colors? Did you use the same kind of pattern? Do the patterns change if you turn the paper strip around?

- Send in your pattern strips, and we will put them together to make a class quilt of patterns. When it's complete, we will be sure to let you know. Please feel free to stop by the classroom and talk with your child about the many different patterns our families have made!

Thank you for helping us learn more about patterns!

Let's Talk About Attributes

Dear Families,

One of things we do each day at school is talk about how things are similar and different. We do this by describing them by their attributes. For example, we notice when children are wearing the same color clothing or when two shapes are different, and when we clean up we put all of the same kind of toy in one basket.

This kind of thinking is important for children, and even though it is simple for adults to sort and compare things, it is something our class is just starting to learn. It helps children at home to know where their toys belong, to be able to take out toys and put them away on their own, and to be able to organize toys by things they have in common.

Here are some ways you can get your child thinking about organizing materials by attributes:

- Keep a lower cabinet in the kitchen filled with plastic storage containers. Children can sort the containers and match them with the correct lids.

- Play a game of sorting lids into groups of small, medium, and big containers. Figuring out which items go together helps your child develop reasoning skills.

- Ask your child to make a pattern with fruits, vegetables, or silverware (for example, carrot, carrot, celery, carrot, carrot, celery). Organizing items in a pattern helps children pay attention to how things are similar and different, which will help them later when they get to algebra!

- Ask children for help sorting clothing while doing the laundry. Matching socks in their pairs is a great way to help children think about how things are the same and different.

- Find patterns in the environment, such as on clothing, in nature, floor tiles, or in art work. Encourage children to identify patterns and describe them.

Your children love patterns, so find as many ways as you can to share in this interest and to help them understand even more about patterns and classifying and the many different ways we use these concepts each day.

Assessing Children's Math Skills—Algebra

What to observe

Children playing games that encourage sorting or matching (e.g., memory matching games, card games where children begin with specific sets of cards)

Children working in the math or manipulative center, using shape sorters, pattern blocks, counting bears, links, and so on

Children in the art area, using materials that encourage sorting or pattern creations

Play in the block area. Children often create patterns with the blocks

Science area activities. Children sort and classify science materials by attributes that are sometimes not as obvious as they are in other play materials

Clean-up time. Children in the block, dramatic play, and manipulatives areas often need to sort materials into the correct containers as they clean up

Music activities that encourage children to listen to and repeat musical patterns or create their own musical patterns

Activities—for individual or group assessment

Sort objects by given attribute (e.g., color, shape, size, animal family)

Create rule for sorting objects and tell about it

Sort objects by function

Older children sort objects by more than one attribute (e.g., sort buttons by color and size)

Ask children to organize materials by a measurement attribute (e.g., shortest to tallest, lightest to heaviest)

Copy given simple pattern (ABABAB)

Extend given simple pattern

Identify patterns in the learning environment

Create patterns (with objects, musical instruments, art materials, etc.)

Example follow-up questions

What do you know about this shape?

Tell me how you knew these shapes were the same/different from these shapes?

Are there other shapes the same/different?

Is there another way you could do the same thing?

How do you know that it's symmetrical/congruent?

Strategies

Focuses on most salient attribute to sort objects

Identifies rule for sorting and checks to see if objects were sorted correctly

Creates and explains own rule for sorting

Uses same attributes to copy pattern (e.g., teacher creates red, blue, red, blue pattern, and child copies the pattern using red and blue)

Uses different attributes to copy pattern but accurately represents the pattern

Individual Evaluation: Assessing Children's Math Skills—Algebra

Date:

Child:

Area of classroom or activity:

Activity used:

Observation notes

Follow-up questions and responses:

Quick summary—Child:
Sorts objects accurately by one attribute
Identifies rule for classified objects
Creates rule for classifying objects
Sorts objects accurately by more than one attribute
Identifies patterns in the environment
Identifies core of simple patterns
Replicates and/or extends simple patterns
Identifies core of more complex patterns
Replicates and/or extends more complex patterns
Creates and identifies new patterns with various materials (art, musical instruments, manipulatives, etc.)
Can extend the counting pattern beyond 29
Can count by 2s or 5s

Developing Geometric and Spatial Thinking Skills

──────────── **FOR THE TEACHER** ────────────

◇ **What You'll Need to Know**

According to the National Research Council (NRC, 2009), preschool children spend the majority of their everyday mathematics experiences focused on geometry and pattern concepts, and research has demonstrated that well-designed activities focused on the development of geometric and spatial skills can be very effective in the early years at building on children's everyday knowledge. Very young children learn to identify basic shapes in the environment and learn vocabulary to define location or movement of themselves or objects, such as "up" and "down." During the preschool years, teachers provide materials and activities that encourage children to explore and identify attributes of shapes and to manipulate and move objects through space. During these experiences, teachers model language for children, adding to their vocabulary with the names of two- and three-dimensional shapes, words used to identify attributes of shapes such as *angle*, *face*, and *symmetrical*, and words used to describe spatial relations. By developing a solid understanding of the concept, understanding the typical developmental trajectory for the concept, and planning activities that intentionally foster that development, teachers prepare to respond to children's natural inclinations in a way that supports and scaffolds their learning.

Curriculum Focal Points (National Council of Teachers of Mathematics [NCTM], 2006) suggests a great deal of content for prekindergarten children in the area of geometry, which is defined for this age as identifying attributes and manipulating shapes and describing spatial relationships. Related expectations for prekindergarten children include the following:

- Recognize, name, build, draw, compare, and sort two- and three-dimensional shapes.

- Describe attributes and parts of two- and three-dimensional shapes.

- Describe, name, and interpret direction and distance in space, and apply ideas about direction and distance.

- Find and name locations with simple relationships such as *near to* in systems such as maps.

- Create mental images of geometric shapes using spatial memory and spatial visualization.

- Recognize geometric shapes and structures in the environment and specify their location.

Kindergarten children learn to identify, name, and describe a variety of shapes, such as trapezoids and parallelograms, and are increasingly able to classify shapes at a more sophisticated level. They also learn to identify three-dimensional shapes such as spheres, cubes, and cylinders and compare and contrast two- and three-dimensional shapes. They use basic shapes and spatial reasoning to model objects in their environment and construct more complex shapes.

The following content expectations (the same or similar to those for prekindergarten) are linked to the kindergarten focal points:

- Recognize, name, build, draw, compare, and sort two- and three-dimensional shapes.

- Describe attributes and parts of two- and three-dimensional shapes.

- Describe, name, and interpret relative positions in space, and apply ideas about relative position.

- Describe, name, and interpret direction and distance in navigating space, and apply ideas about direction and distance.

- Find and name locations with simple relationships such as *near to.*

- Create mental images of geometric shapes using spatial memory and spatial visualization.

- Recognize geometric shapes and structures in the environment and specify their location.

Children learn through exploring their world; thus, their interests and everyday activities are natural vehicles for developing mathematical thinking. Shapes are all around us! Children learn early to be shape detectives at home, in the classroom, and on walking trips outside.

Yet, without good experiences, children rely on what is often inadequate exposure to and experiences with geometry, limiting their understanding to simple prototypes and misguided conclusions. Teachers will want to take advantage of everyday encounters with shape and space, but they will also want to build on children's knowledge by intentionally planning explorations with problems, materials, and children's books that facilitate emergent concepts of geometry. Rather than spending the majority of time asking children to repeat what they already know (Thomas, 1982), teachers must be prepared to expand on and build on children's knowledge by presenting unique challenges, new experiences, and new and interesting materials.

◇ Key Concepts

- Geometric shapes can be two- or three-dimensional.

- Two- and three-dimensional geometric shapes can be defined and classified by unique and/or shared attributes.

- Children learn about attributes by composing and decomposing shapes

- Spatial orientation means understanding where you are physically in the world and how to get around it. Children learn math through their navigation of space.

- Spatial visualization allows children to cognitively manipulate shapes and images.

◇ Goals and Objectives

- Children will recognize, name, and identify attributes of two- and three-dimensional shapes.

- Children will compose new shapes from two- and/or three-dimensional shapes.

- Children will compare, contrast, and classify two- and three-dimensional shapes.

- Children will represent two- and three-dimensional shapes.

- Children will describe and name relative positions in space with simple language such as *beside*, *above*, and *below.*

- Children will communicate ideas about direction and location.

- Children will represent spaces with physical models, pictures, and symbols.

◇ **What You'll Need**

In order to provide children with developmentally appropriate experiences and relevant vocabulary, teachers need to refresh their memories of a subject they may not have considered since their sophomore year in high school. There are several appropriate geometry books available that will give teachers confidence to teach these concepts in their classrooms and will help them plan appropriate assessments and activities for all young children. One helpful book is *Navigating Through Geometry in Prekindergarten–Grade 2 (with CD-Rom)* (Findell et al., 2001). Like its companion book in algebra (Greenes, Cavanagh, Dacey, Findell, & Small, 2001), it demonstrates how some basic ideas of geometry can be introduced, developed, and extended. It deals with two- and three-dimensional shapes and introduces methods to describe location and position.

Other books that may be helpful are these:

Clements, D. H., & Sarama, J. (2009). *Learning and Teaching Early Math: The Learning Trajectories Approach*. In addition to substantial information on the development of number concepts, this book dedicates three chapters to the development of spatial thinking and understanding of shapes. Typical learning and development trajectories for children birth to age 8 are provided, along with suggestions for instructional tasks.

Gerdes, P. (1999). *Geometry from Africa: Mathematical and Educational Explorations*. The author shows how geometrical ideas are manifested in the work of African artisans. The large number of beautiful illustrations may inspire young artists to link their art with emergent concepts of geometry.

Orlando, L. (1993). *The Multicultural Game Book*. This book includes ideas for shapes that children can make and geometric principles they can learn from games.

NCTM (2009). *Understanding Geometry for a Changing World*. This book includes lessons, activities sheets, and a CD with additional information and video clips.

Children's Books

Blackstone, S. (2009). *Bear in a Square/Oso en un Cuadrado*.

Burns, M. (1994). *The Greedy Triangle*.

Carle, E. (1986). *The Secret Birthday Message*.

Diehl, D. (2007). *A Circle Here, a Square There*.

Dodds, D. A. (1994). *The Shape of Things*.

Greene, R. G. (2001). *When a Line Bends . . . A Shape Begins*.

Grifalconi, V. (1986). *The Village of Round and Square Houses*.

Grover, M. (1996). *Circles and Squares Everywhere*.

Hirst, R., & Hirst, S. (1990). *My Place in Space*.

Hoban, T. (1986). *Shapes, Shapes, Shapes*.

Hoban, T. (1996). *Circles, Triangles, and Squares*.

Hoban, T. (2000). *Cubes, Cones, Cylinders, and Spheres*.

Rissman, R. (2009). *Shapes in Buildings (Spot the Shape)*.

Rissman, R. (2009). *Shapes in Art (Spot the Shape)*.

Santomero, A. C. (1998). *The Shape Detectives*.

Serfozo, M. (1996). *There's a Square: A Book About Shapes*.

Shaw, C. G. (1988). *It Looked Like Spilt Milk*.

Seuss, Dr. (1988). *The Shape of Me and Other Stuff*.

Staake, B. (2006). *The Red Lemon*.

Silverstein, S. (1976). *The Missing Piece*.

Tompert, A. (1997). *Grandfather Tang's Story*.

Other Things You'll Need

- Containers for sorting

- Many types of blocks, including wooden, hollow, homemade, and/or foam and in interesting shapes such as arcs, cylinders, and triangular prisms

- A protected space designated for construction, large enough for several children to build independent structures at the same time

- Small three-dimensional shapes and blocks in various shapes for building, sorting, and manipulating

- Paper, drawing tools, collage materials, pipe cleaners, three-dimensional art supplies such as paper towel rolls, milk cartons, and tissue paper boxes, play dough molds

- Magazines, newspaper, and catalogs for creating collages or covering three-dimensional artwork

- Puzzles with varying levels of difficulty

- Shape-sorting toys, including boxes with holes for different shapes, seriated shape sorters, nesting arcs or cups, shape bingo

- Magnetized shapes

- Journals and clipboards for children to record observations

- Digital camera for taking pictures of children's constructions

- Geoboards with bands

- A set of tangrams for older children

- Pattern blocks to compose and decompose shapes

 ### The Home–School Connection

The Early Childhood Learning and Knowledge Center (http://eclkc.ohs.acf.hhs.gov/hslc) provides many resources for parents and teachers to help them support mathematics at home. Their helpful guides for families provide clear, simple activities caregivers can do during daily routines that support children's learning. Through simple newsletters, bulletin boards, and special events at school, teachers can convey more specific strategies for developing emergent geometry concepts and skills throughout the day. Things that parents can do to help their children learn geometry include the following:

- Talk about shapes that are seen each day at home, running errands, or on the way to and from school. With younger children, family members can identify shapes by name and ask children to find other, similar shapes. With older children, parents can play "I Spy" and have children guess the shape from several clues.

- Allow children to create new play spaces, such as under the dining room table or making a tent with chairs and blankets.

- Use descriptive vocabulary when cleaning up or organizing, such as, "I will put away these round ones and you can put away the square and rectangle ones." Organizing playthings at home also helps children develop spatial thinking as they determine whether spaces are the right size for objects.

- Provide containers and boxes of different sizes for children to play with. Hands-on experiences provide opportunities for concrete explorations of shape concepts.

- At the playground, create an obstacle course for a young child or ask an older child to create the obstacle course and direct family members through it using words like *under*, *over*, *through*, and *on top of*.

- Outside, observe interesting and unique shapes in nature: compare leaves and shapes of rocks, observe the different ways water puddles on the ground, and manipulate shadows with hand and body movements.

Once parents and families are aware of the many opportunities that arise each day to talk about shape and space, they will begin to see how naturally curious their children are to explore the many geometric and spatial concepts the world has to offer. The tear-out sheets on page 114 are sample letters for parents, with suggested activities.

◇ Documenting and Assessing Children's Learning

Assessing children's emergent understanding of geometry and spatial thinking will be a continuous activity done on an individual and group basis. Teachers will utilize the following:

- Observations of children's explorations and conversations

- Small and large group discussions with students as they work individually and in groups

- Structured interviews with students

- Portfolios of children's work collected throughout the year

- Children's self-evaluations, drawings, and dictated stories about geometry concepts

- Specific tasks or activities designed to discover information about children's knowledge

Chapters 1, 9, and 10 have many examples of ways in which teachers can document and assess children's learning. All types of charts, diagrams, graphs, and other visual representations give children the ability to review the data they have collected and reach conclusions. Teachers will observe children's understanding of concepts of geometry as they watch them communicate their findings to others. They will further use individual portfolios to keep examples of children's work at intervals during the school year, so that progress in their understanding of emergent concepts of geometry may be gauged.

The tear-out sheets on pages 114–115 at the end of this chapter are guides to help you better understand children's development and to help plan for future instruction. These guides are not meant to be used as occasional "tests" of children's knowledge; they should be used as references for what to observe and document during informal interactions and more organized activities. It is also important to be reflective about what the assessment information tells you about each child and whether your documentation indicates clearly whether they understand a concept and are ready to move on or need more guidance. In addition to concepts children should learn, the guides include topical questions and suggestions teachers can use in different learning areas to elicit responses from children that demonstrate their understanding of shape and space.

As teachers document children's development, they will want to share the experiences with the class, with other members of the school community, and with parents. Taking pictures of what children have constructed allows them and other children to view their structures from different perspectives. Connecting these pictures to narratives of the children's strategies as well as specific skills learned while building validates their work and teaches families more about what children are learning each day as they play. This kind of documentation also allows children to revisit favorite structures, improve on them, recreate them, or compare them to new structures.

FOR THE CHILDREN

Teachers recognize that young children experience geometry spontaneously in their lives and in their play. Children make sense of the world around them by exploring shapes and patterns, drawing and creating geometric designs, and learning new vocabulary to name the things they see. Through the following active experiences, children can build on the strengths and interests that are already present.

According to the National Research Council (2009) and the new *Common Core Standards*, after number and operations, geometry is an essential concept for children to learn and master in the early years. The *Principles and Standards for School Mathematics* (NCTM, 2000) recommends that students use their notions of geometric ideas to become more proficient in describing, representing, and navigating their environment. They should learn to represent two- and three-dimensional shapes through drawings, block constructions, dramatizations, and words. They should explore shapes by decomposing them and creating new ones. Their knowledge of direction and position should be refined through the use of spoken language to locate objects and by giving and following multistep directions.

Many of the following activities can be done with children in small or large groups and then left out as part of learning areas for children to explore on their own during active learning times.

◇ Exploring Geometry

1. Children Explore Shapes

◆ Finding and naming shapes. Working with children in a small group, present two sets of basic shapes, in varying colors. From one set, take a shape and ask a child to find the exact same shape in a different color from the other set. Once the child finds the shape, ask her to tell you what the shape is. With older children, include more complex and irregular shapes and hold them up in varying orientations. Dual language learners and children with language delays will be able to participate fully in this activity while you assist them with learning the names for the shapes.

◆ Feely box. With this activity, teachers place different shapes into a box or bag, and children reach in and choose one but do not take it out of the box. With younger children, they can simply identify the shape. Older children can give clues to friends about the attributes of the shape and have them guess what it is. Starting with basic shapes allows children to master the descriptive skills, and gradually adding new, more complex shapes challenges all children to think more abstractly about shapes and their properties. Dual language learners or children who have language delays can work with the teacher or teammate to provide clues to friends.

◆ Guess my rule (Clements & Sarama, 2009). Slowly sort pattern blocks or other shapes into two groups by a specific rule and ask children to guess what the rule is. As you sort, some children will begin to guess the rule, and you can allow them to quietly point to the pile where the next shape should go. Simple rules at first will work best, such as circles and squares, or squares and rectangles, and the piles should differ by only one attribute. As the year progresses, the rules can become more challenging, such as squares and not squares, or four sides and three sides.

◆ Hexagon bingo. Provide children with sheets of paper showing the outlines of six pattern-block-sized hexagons. Create a large die out of a milk carton or other light cube and place images of pattern block shapes on each side (triangle, trapezoid, rhombus, hexagon). As children take turns rolling the die, they choose the correct piece and add it to any one of their hexagon outlines. Children continue until all shapes are filled in. With older children, the die can be changed to include attributes (e.g., four sides, parallelogram, two equal angles) or shapes can be added that do not fit correctly into the hexagon outline, such as the square or elongated rhombus. In mixed-age group settings, pair older children with younger children to encourage teamwork.

◆ Read *The Shape Detectives* by Angela Santomero. Go on a shape walk. Have the children act as "shape detectives" and record the shapes they observe and where they were found. The teacher can assist as necessary by providing clues and helping children to record their findings. Be sure to take along clipboards or journals for children to draw or write their findings. Then graph or chart how many of each shape the children found. Ask children to look for shapes on their way home and their way back to school the next day. When children arrive the next morning, they can place their name on a chart labeled "Did you see a shape on your way?" with sections for shapes such as circles, squares, triangles, and hexagons.

◆ Shape pictures. In the art area, provide many different types of construction paper shapes or outlines of shapes for children to cut. Each day, children can make pictures with shapes using different suggestions, such as "Make a picture using only 3 shapes," or "Only use shapes with 4 sides," or "Make one big shape out of many little shapes."

◆ Food shapes. Fruits and vegetables are some of the few geometric objects that can actually be cut in half to see what happens. Take advantage of this by having children observe and describe fruits such as oranges or grapes and vegetables such as cucumbers or carrots, and then as you cut them into pieces, have children describe new shapes they observe. This encourages children to consider part-whole relationships, as well as the connection between two- and three-dimensional shapes. Later, have children recall their experience by drawing the shapes they "discovered" inside the fruits and vegetables or classifying pictures of the fruits and vegetables on a chart.

◆ Read *The Yellow Lemon* by Bob Staakes. Ask children to identify shapes they observe in the illustrations. Using real lemons, have children describe them before

Children read The Yellow Lemon and explore their classroom for shapes.

and after cutting them open. Discuss the ways lemons are similar to or different from other fruits you have explored. Make some lemonade!

◆ Shape constructor. Provide children with straws, coffee stirrers, or ice pop sticks cut to various lengths. Encourage them to create new shapes using a certain number or specific lengths of straws. Make sure the points of the straws are touching at each corner. Encourage children to create shapes that look different with the same number of straws.

◆ Read *Shapes, Shapes, Shapes* and *Circles, Triangles, and Squares* by Tana Hoban. Have children identify the shapes on each page of the book. Chart their answers. They will probably have trouble discriminating among these complex patterns at first. Ask them to look closely for more shapes. Have children write a story about one of the books. Ask them to use "shape words" such as *circle*, *hexagon*, *oval*, *rhombus*, *rectangle*, *square*, and *triangle*. There are some surprising shapes in the photographs. Suggest they may want to use *heart*, *arc*, or *star* in the story.

◆ Treasure hunt. Give children paper bags (one for each) and ask them to find things of a certain shape that you have put around the room or outside. They may also find shapes in nature to bring into the classroom and exhibit.

2. Children Investigate Shapes, Maps, and Space

◆ Stamp art prints. Provide children each with the same size piece of paper and various materials to dip into paint, such as milk cartons, paper towel rolls, sponges, and play dough molds. Have children try to fill up as much of their page as they can without allowing the shapes to touch. Smaller objects such as quarters or dice may be used with older children to encourage development of fine motor skills as well.

◆ Hot and cold. While one child covers his eyes, hide a small bear or dog somewhere in the classroom. As the child takes steps to find the bear, ask children to tell him if he's "hot" and moving closer to the object or "cold" and moving away. Encourage children to give hints using directional words such as "It's *near* the bookshelf," "It's hiding *under* something," or "Look *behind* the door." Pair younger or dual language children with older or English-speaking children to help them find the bear successfully. Use hand and body motions to convey the meanings of positional words.

◆ Play a variation of Simon Says with bean bags and using position words (for instance, Simon says put your bean bag "above your head," "behind your back," "on top of a shelf"). Have children try out as many space words as they can. Examples are *near/far, in/out, in front of/behind, next to/beside,* and *above/below.*

◆ Felt maps. Ask children to think about the playground and what kinds of things are there, such as the fence, the swing, or the garden box. Take a walk around the playground, emphasizing where things are in relation to each other and in relation to the entrance to the playground. After your walk, encourage children to represent the playground on a felt board with shapes cut to represent individual parts. Discuss the relationship between locations of felt pieces to actual locations of things on the playground. Take the felt board outside to check for accuracy. Older children may attempt to draw images of the playground and perhaps do the same for the classroom as well.

◆ Hide and seek. Using the felt map or drawings of maps, place an object in one location on the map and ask children to find it where it has been hidden in the actual playground.

◆ Block play. Provide a well-equipped block area with blocks of all kinds and labeled shelves on which to sort them when play is over. Blocks should be sorted on shelves by type, and the outline of each shape should be on the shelf to guide children as they return materials. Give children plenty of time to create complex block play and allow older children to work on structures for more than a day at a time. Add accessories to enhance play, including street signs, play people, animals, different types of vehicles, different types of small building or connecting blocks, paper and pencils with clipboards, and books about architecture and construction. See the tear-out sheets on pages 116–117 for examples of questions to ask children to encourage geometry and spatial thinking.

When children play with interesting shapes, they begin to understand shape attributes as well as how to move shapes through space to create new shapes.

◇ Reflecting

In order for children to learn from their experiences, it is important to encourage them to reflect on their accomplishments, problems they may have encountered, and strategies they used to solve problems. Documenting children's experiences also validates their time in the class and builds a sense of community among all of the learners. Provide children with spaces to display their work, including three-dimensional displays of art or block constructions. Take pictures of children working and allow them to take pictures of their own work. Ask them to dictate or write about what they were thinking and doing during the experience. Other members of the school community and families should be invited frequently to participate in this shared reflection.

Have an open house for family members to experiment with active math experiences involving two- and three-dimensional shapes and spatial thinking. Many of the games and activities listed here can be set up for small groups of families and children to play together. Designate older students as leaders of the small groups, explaining the rules and making sure families understand how the activities work. Be sure to have your reading center well stocked with children's books relating to mathematics for family members to read with children.

◇ Extending and Expanding to the Primary Grades

For Grade 1

The curriculum focal point for grade 1 geometry is composing and decomposing geometric shapes (NCTM, 2006). Although children have explored this concept in preschool and kindergarten, first graders are capable of thinking about shape composition at a much more advanced level. Children build complex towers with multiple levels, create shapes and images out of smaller shapes and duplicate shapes made from other shapes, and become more flexible in their thinking shape composition. Related expectations in geometry for grade 1 are for children to master these skills:

- Recognize, name, build, draw, compare, and sort two- and three-dimensional shapes.

- Describe attributes and parts of two- and three-dimensional shapes.

- Investigate and predict the results of putting together and taking apart two- and three-dimensional shapes.

- Recognize and create shapes that have symmetry.

- Create mental images of geometric shapes using spatial memory and spatial visualization.

- Recognize and represent shapes from different perspectives.

- Recognize geometric shapes and structures in the environment and specify their location.

For Grade 2

Geometry is not considered a curriculum focal point for grade 2. It is connected, however, to the focal points for measurement. Children use geometric measurement to estimate, measure, and compute lengths as they solve problems involving data, space, and movement through space. By composing and decomposing two-dimensional shapes (intentionally substituting arrangements of smaller shapes for larger shapes or substituting larger shapes for many smaller shapes), they use geometric knowledge and spatial reasoning to develop foundations for understanding area, fractions, and proportions.

Related expectations for grade 2 include the following:

- Describe, name, and interpret direction and distance in navigating space and apply ideas about direction and distance.

- Relate ideas in geometry to ideas in number and measurement.

For Grade 3

The curriculum focal point for grade 3 geometry is describing and analyzing properties of two-dimensional shapes. Related expectations include the following:

- Identify, compare, and analyze attributes of two- and three-dimensional shapes and develop vocabulary to describe the attributes.

- Classify two- and three-dimensional shapes according to their properties, and develop definitions of classes of shapes such as triangles and pyramids.

- Investigate, describe, and reason about the results of subdividing, combining, and transforming shapes.

- Explore congruence and similarity.

- Make and test conjectures about geometric properties and relationships and develop logical arguments to justify conclusions.

- Make and use coordinate systems to specify locations and to describe paths.

- Build and draw geometric objects.

- Create and describe mental images of objects, patterns, and paths.

- Use geometric models to solve problems in other areas of mathematics, such as number and measurement.

- Recognize geometric ideas and relationships and apply them to other disciplines and to problems that arise in the classroom or in everyday life.

Children in the early primary grades can do the following:

- Use interactive computer programs for activities in which students put together or take apart shapes. The National Council of Teachers of Mathematics has electronic examples that can be used for different age groups (see Resources list at the end of this book). One interactive sequence is called "Investigating the Concept of Triangle and Properties of Polygons." It uses interactive geoboards to help students identify shapes, describe their properties, and develop spatial sense. In the second part, students make and compare various polygons, describing the properties of the shapes they create.

- Identify a wide variety of shapes and nonshapes embedded in other shapes.

- Apply transformations and use symmetry to analyze mathematical situations. Students can recognize and create shapes that have symmetry and recognize and apply slides, flips, and turns in shapes. They can use pattern blocks to create designs with line and rotational symmetry or paper cutouts, paper folding, and mirrors to investigate symmetry. To strengthen spatial reasoning abilities, the teacher can provide predetermined shapes and ask children to determine which pattern blocks fit most effectively within the confines of the shape.

Children can use geoboards to explore attributes of shapes and to observe how their actions change the properties of the shapes.

- Explore geometric properties by composing or decomposing units of units (shapes made from other shapes).

- Refine and extend concepts of position in space by developing map skills that include making route maps and using simple coordinates to locate the school on a city map. Some computer programs allow students to navigate through mazes or maps.

- Replicate or identify different configurations of shapes from memory.

- Develop some sense of perspective as children draw structures that they have built with small boxes. The teacher can collect (with the help of parents) boxes of various sizes and shapes such as jewelry boxes, shoe boxes, and cereal boxes. The children can then use the boxes to build structures. They later can try to draw what they see when looking at the structures they have created. If they have trouble with the drawing segment of the activity, the teacher can encourage them to draw part of the structure.

- Think more abstractly about shape concepts. For example, children can read *The Greedy Triangle* by Marilyn Burns. In this story about a triangle that is unhappy with its shape and keeps asking the local Shapeshifter to give it more sides and angles, there are many important jobs for triangles, quadrilaterals, pentagons, and hexagons. Let students choose which of the four they would like to be and explain orally and in writing the reasons for their choice. Continue building vocabulary by adding terms to a word wall or chart.

- Understand that shapes have their background in historical tradition, folktales, and ancient cultures. For example, tangrams are ancient Chinese puzzle pieces of geometric shapes still used today by adults and children to design beautiful and unique pictures. A good book to accompany an experience with tangrams is

Grandfather Tang's Story by Ann Tompert. In this multicultural, intergenerational story, seven "tans" (traditional pieces of a square) are arranged and rearranged to represent various characters in the story. There is a traceable tangram at the end, which can be used to create endless classroom projects.

- Appreciate the beauty of a poem about shapes. Read *The Missing Piece* by Shel Silverstein to young elementary school students. Discuss the possibility that everyone needs something to make them whole (a better person, a smarter person, and so on). Have children discuss what they might be missing and what they could do to find their missing piece.

- Build a larger and more complex vocabulary pertaining to geometric and spatial concepts.

- Learn more complex classification systems for two- and three-dimensional shapes.

Exploring Geometry in our Classroom!

Dear Families,

We have been talking a lot about geometry in our classroom and exploring many different ways to use geometry. We wanted to let you know how we learn about geometry as we play each day.

Block Area

When we play with blocks, we learn about geometry because the blocks are 3-dimensional, meaning they have height, width, and depth. Our blocks come in many different shapes and sizes, and we learn how squares and circles are similar to and different from cubes and cylinders. We also love to put blocks together to make new shapes and sometimes notice that some shapes balance differently than others and some are easier to stack than others.

Art

When we work in the art area, we aren't just making a mess, we are learning how to make shapes with paint and paint brushes, with play dough, and by cutting them out of construction paper. We use collage materials that come in different shapes and we create many different designs with them. When we use art materials such as tissue boxes, paper towel rolls, and egg cartons to create 3-dimensional art, we learn more about how shapes go together to make new shapes.

Small Toy Area

There are many different kinds of toys in this area that teach us about geometry. Inch cubes, different colored shapes, and small building blocks help us think about how shapes are the same and different. Geoboards help us think about how to make shapes bigger or smaller by moving the rubber bands and what makes a square different from a rectangle or triangle. We also love shape puzzles, which help us learn shape names and think about fitting shapes into the correct spaces.

These are just a few of our learning areas, but we are learning about geometry in all areas of our classroom! Here are some things you can do to help us think about geometry at home:

- Talk about shapes in the environment. Go on a "shape hunt" and find different shapes in your house or on the way to school.

- When you talk about shapes, use words that describe them such as, "It has three sides," or "It's round and smooth," or "I see four points on the square *and* on the rectangle."

- Recycle materials like cereal boxes or yogurt cups and allow your child to build structures with them.

Did You See a Shape on Your Way?

We have been talking a lot about geometry in our classroom and exploring many different ways to use geometry. We wanted to ask you to help us think more about shapes when we aren't at school.

Next week, each child will share with the class whether they saw a shape on their way to school. We will write our responses on a chart, along with the object or shape that each child saw on the way to school. So, please remember to look for shapes this week as you walk or drive to school, or remind your child to look for a shape before leaving for school.

You can do this as a family at home, keeping track of shapes you may have seen on your way home from school or work. If you'd like to share your results with us, we'd love to see them!

As always, if you would like to participate further in our exploration of shapes, please feel free to contact me about coming in to do a special art project with shapes, to play with us in the block area, to read a book about shapes, or to contribute some materials to the class.

We can also always use interesting recycled materials to help us create new shapes in the art area, so if you have any of the following, please send them in.

empty cereal/ food boxes	empty tissue boxes	clean, empty yogurt containers
cardboard egg cartons	packing styrofoam	shoe boxes
Clay	toothpicks	clean, empty juice boxes
wooden dowels	wood glue	tape

Thank you!

Assessing Children's Math Skills—Geometry

What to observe

Children playing games that encourage shape identification, such as shape bingo, pattern block mats, or shape sorters

Children working in the math or manipulative center, using shape sorters, pattern blocks, small building blocks, tangrams, and so on

Children in the art area, using materials that encourage creation of two- and three-dimensional shapes, such as play-dough molds, collage materials, and three-dimensional art materials

Play in the block area. This is where children are most encouraged to explore attributes of three-dimensional shapes

Children playing computer games that encourage thinking about and creating two- and three-dimensional shapes

Clean-up time. Children in the block area demonstrate their understanding of shape properties by returning blocks to the correct places on the shelf

Activities—for individual or group assessment

Identify two- and three-dimensional shapes

Compare two- and three-dimensional shapes by similarities/differences in attributes

Use sense of touch to feel shapes and describe them by their attributes

Turn, flip, and combine shapes to create new shapes

Use geoboards to create symmetrical or congruent shapes

Use the smallest/largest amount of attribute blocks to fill in a certain space

Build different three-dimensional structures using the same set of blocks

Example follow-up questions

What do you know about this shape?

Tell me how you knew these shapes were the same/different from these shapes?

How did you know these shapes would fit together?

Are there other shapes the same/different?

Is there another way you could do the same thing?

How do you know that they are symmetrical/congruent?

Strategies:

Turns shapes to identify them

Uses two-dimensional names to identify three-dimensional objects

Uses information about known shape attributes to identify/discuss unknown shapes

Rotates and puts together shapes to create new shapes

Uses shapes to solve problems

Solves puzzles by using attributes of puzzle pieces to guess where pieces belong

Individual Evaluation: Assessing Children's Math Skills—Geometry

Date:

Child:

Area of classroom or activity:

Activity used:

Observation notes

Follow-up questions and responses:

Quick summary—Child:
Finds shapes in the environment
Names two-dimensional basic shapes (circle, square, rectangle, triangle)
Names less common shapes (hexagon, trapezoid, parallelogram)
Names three-dimensional shapes
Describes attributes of two- and three-dimensional shapes
Compares two- and three-dimensional shapes
Builds with two- and three-dimensional shapes
Turns and flips shapes to fit them into the correct spaces
Combines shapes to create new shapes
Identifies symmetrical shapes
Creates symmetrical shapes
Identifies congruent shapes

8

Learning the Basic Concepts
of Measurement

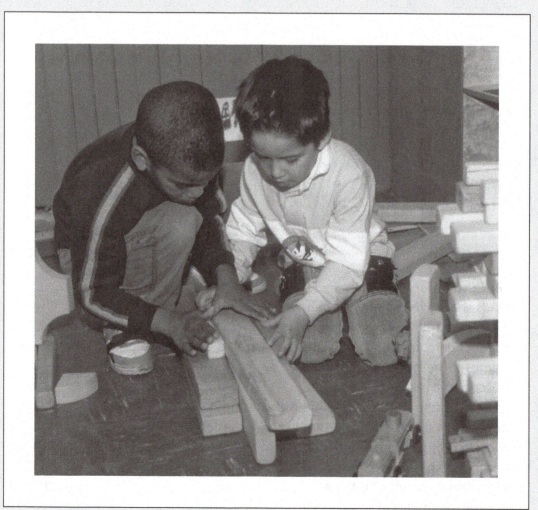

FOR THE TEACHER

◇ **What You'll Need to Know**

Measurement is a concept that ties together the two other main mathematical domains of geometry and number. Because of this connection, young children's experiences with measurement provide them with information about more than just length and width, but about area, shape, and number patterns and relationships. Children encounter and discuss measurement concepts daily (Seo & Ginsburg, 2004). There are many opportunities in everyday experiences for children to compare and contrast sizes of things, to determine how much of something they need, to share materials so everyone has some, to pour just enough milk into a cup. They also encounter measurement concepts as they play with materials provided to guide exploration of measurement, such as different-sized containers in the sand; water tables, inch cubes, and pegs and peg boards in the manipulatives center; different sizes of unit blocks in the block area; and measuring cups and spoons in the dramatic play area. These materials lead to questions about measurement. How many small cups of water do I need to fill the bucket? Do we have the same amounts of clay? Is my tower the same size as yours? Young children are infinitely interested in finding the answers to the many questions they have about things that can be measured, such as their own height and weight.

In the early childhood years, children begin to understand measurement in terms of what they know such as labeling things that are small, medium, big as baby, mommy, and daddy (Clements & Sarama, 2009). They begin to use measurement language such as *more*, *big*, *little*, and compare two objects directly to figure out if they are equal. Preschool children should (1) begin to understand the measurable attributes of objects and (2) be able to choose and apply techniques and tools to find out the answers to questions of measurement. They begin by looking at, touching, or directly comparing objects. Teachers will want to guide students by providing the resources for measuring, planning formal and informal opportunities to measure, encouraging students to explain and discuss their findings, and asking important questions to facilitate their thinking and concept development.

The National Council of Teachers of Mathematics (NCTM, 2000) suggests, in the measurement standard for grades preK–2, that measurement is one of the most widely used applications of mathematics. For young children, informal measurement experiences teach important everyday skills and also develop measurement concepts and processes that will be formalized and expanded in later years. A foundation in measurement concepts involves direct hands-on experiences with comparing objects, counting units of measurement (both formal and informal), and using a variety of tools. The NCTM takes the position that schools should teach both the metric and customary systems of measurement at this time and develop children's ability to solve problems in either system.

Curriculum focal points (NCTM, 2006) for prekindergarten suggest that measurement for this age group involves identifying measurable attributes and comparing objects by using these attributes. Children identify objects as "the same" or "different" and "more" or "less" on the basis of attributes that they can measure, such as length and weight. They notice large differences in size and shape and solve problems by making direct comparisons of objects on the basis of those attributes. Related expectations for prekindergarten measurement include the following:

• Recognize the attributes of length, volume, weight, and area.

• Compare and order objects according to these attributes.

Kindergarten-aged children use measurable attributes, such as length and weight, to solve problems by comparing and ordering objects. They compare the lengths of two objects both directly and indirectly (by comparing both with a third object). They order several objects according to length. The related expectations for kindergarten children are the same as those for prekindergarten.

Young children have difficulty with the concept of time. Although some young children will learn to tell time, they have egocentric beliefs about time that hinder the development of basic concepts, such as the notion that time intervals are not constant—that they can catch up with their brother in age—or that someone is older because they are taller. Rather than learning to tell time, young children should be exposed to time concepts as they occur naturally, such as the progression through minutes, hours, days, weeks, and months. The daily and weekly classroom schedules require teachers to discuss time as it relates directly to children, such as "school days" and "home days" and "Five more minutes before we go inside and have lunch." When basic concepts of time are tied to concrete things or experiences, children begin to understand them.

Measurement of length is similarly abstract, in that there are rules for measurement that adults take for granted but young children will not be able to grasp for some time. This includes understanding that some things change in size while others remain static. In order to be reliable, measurement units must be the same and comparisons must be made by the same attribute. Although measurement concepts are in some ways easy to teach, they pose a challenge for young children because of their abstract nature. Young learners have particular difficulty in making the transition from informal to more formal understandings, so it is essential to provide a solid conceptual foundation through many diverse experiences that will help ease the transition.

◇ Key Concepts

- Things may be compared with respect to length, area, capacity, and weight.

- Objects may be ordered according to these attributes.

- Length concepts involve *how long*, *how high*, *how far*, and *how wide*.

- Area concepts require that children look at more than one measurable dimension.

- Capacity and volume have many everyday applications, as with sand and water.

- Weight can be measured and compared using balance scales or regular scales.

- Time is relative for young children and is best taught through everyday routines and conversations.

- Measurement varies with the size of the unit used to make the measurement.

- Accurate measurement depends on proper use of an appropriate tool.

◇ Goals and Objectives

Goals and objectives for young children in the area of measurement involve both understandings and applications. According to NCTM (2002), depending on the age of the child, instructional programs for young children in grades preK–2 should enable all students to do the following:

- Understand measurable attributes of objects and the units, systems, and processes of measurement.

- Apply appropriate techniques, tools, and formulas to determine measurements. (Whereas adults know instinctively that they will need a scale to measure weight or an egg timer to measure time, young children have not had sufficient experiences with the tools of measurement to make correct choices.)

Thus, in the math program for young children, activities will be formulated to help children to begin to do the following:

- Children will recognize the attributes of length, volume, weight, and area.

- Children will compare and order objects according to these attributes.

- Children will begin to understand how to measure things using standard and/or nonstandard units.

- Children will be able to select the appropriate unit and tool for the attribute being measured.

- Children will measure with multiple copies of units of the same size, such as long unit blocks.

- Children will use repetition of a single unit to measure something larger than the unit.

- Children will use standard tools such as rulers and scales to measure.

- Children will learn a beginning measurement vocabulary.

- Children will use measurement to solve everyday school and home problems.

Length measurement receives the most emphasis in the early childhood classroom. Length concepts involve *how long*, *how high*, *how far*, *how wide*, and *how far around* something is—but young children are also interested in other measurable attributes of objects, and they require meaningful opportunities to use all measurable attributes in order to form a comprehensive foundation for learning concepts of measurement.

◇ What You'll Need

There are some activity books that contain measurement experiences to help with in-depth, concept-building experiences for young children. The following may be helpful, and activities for kindergartners may be adapted for younger preschool children:

Andrews, A. G., & Trafton, P. R. (2002). *Little Kids, Powerful Problem Solvers: Math Stories from a Kindergarten Classroom.* One story describes the first lesson in a year-long focus on measurement as a theme. The goal is for children to make sense of mathematics by rooting it in concrete experiences, such as by using rice and water to investigate capacity and examine the behavior of liquids and solids.

Burns, M. (1993). *Math and Literature (K–3).* This book has a very good lesson on measurement using *How Big Is a Foot?* by Rolf Myller.

Charlesworth, R. (2012). *Experiences in Math for Young Children.* The author covers fundamental concepts and skills for prekindergarten through grade 3. There is a section on measurement that is tied to the NCTM standards.

Patilla, P. (1999). *Math Links Series: Measuring.* This books links measurement with everyday occurrences. The left-hand page introduces the concept, and the right-hand page shows the concept at work in the real world. The teacher will appreciate the glossary and reference list for further reading.

Payne, J. N. (Ed.). (1990). *Mathematics for the Young Child.* Activities and suggestions are presented for teacher educators and teachers in preschool through grade 4.

Children's Books

Adler, D. A. (1999). *How Tall, How Short, How Faraway.*

Anno, M. (1987). *Anno's Math Games.*

Carle, E. (1969). *The Very Hungry Caterpillar.*

Carle, E. (1996). *The Grouchy Ladybug.*

Fowler, R. (1993). *Ladybug on the Move.*

Hoban, T. (1985). *Is It Larger? Is It Smaller?*

Hopkins, L. B. (Ed.). (1997). *Marvelous Math: A book of Poems.*

Hutchins, P. (1970). *Clocks and More Clocks.*

Jenkins, S. (1996). *Biggest, Strongest, Fastest.*

Jenkins, S. (2004). *Actual Size.*

Krauss, R. (2004). *The Carrot Seed.*

Leoni, L. (2001). *Inch by Inch.*

Leedy, L. (2000). *Measuring Penny.*

Meeks, S. (2002). *Drip Drop.*

Murphy, S. (1997). *Betcha!*

Myller, R. (1991). *How Big Is a Foot?*

Pinczes, E. J. (2001). *Inchworm and a Half.*

Schwartz, D. M. (1985). *How Much Is a Million?*

Scieszka, J., & Smith, L. (1995). *Math Curse.*

Shaw, C. G. (1988). *It Looked Like Spilt Milk.*

Tompert, A. (1996). *Just a Little Bit.*

Wing, R. W. (1963). *What Is Big?*

Other Things You'll Need

- Nonstandard units of measurement such as lengths of string, blocks, and links

- Standard units of measurement such as metric and customary rulers, tape measures, tablespoons, various sizes of containers (quart and so on), cups of various sizes, different types of scales (bathroom, balance—a two-sided scale that has containers on either side—and kitchen)

- Art materials such as varying lengths of string, different-sized pom-poms or other collage materials, three-dimensional materials to build with, mural or easel paper, and paints in gradually changing shades of color

- Water, sand, rice, clay, and other materials to work with volume

- Different types of timers such as digital, egg timers, and plastic minute hourglasses

- Math journals

- Construction paper, chart paper, markers, paper plates, fasteners, and other art materials

- Objects for weighing—including objects that vary not only in weight but size as well, smaller objects that are heavy and larger objects that are light, and objects from indoors or outdoors

- Cooking tools such as measuring cups and spoons

- Clear containers full of materials in different sizes such as marbles or coins for children to sort and compare

- Small building materials such as inch cubes, bristle blocks, pegs and peg boards, and small wooden blocks

 ## The Home–School Connection

In its booklet on early mathematics (Fromboluti, Rinck, Magarity, & Gibson, 1999), the U.S. Department of Education has many suggestions for practicing measurement with children. Teachers can convey these ideas and others to families through newsletters, bulletin boards, meetings, and special school activities. The tear-out sheets on pages 132 and 133 provide sample newsletters. Another excellent source of activities is the Family Math Program at the University of California. Its book *Family Math for Young Children: Comparing* (Stenmark & Coates, 1997) provides many suggestions for activities involving measuring and comparing attributes. The following are some ideas for families:

- Keep a record of children's height by marking the wall lightly with erasable pencil or posting a height chart and measuring height every month. Young children love seeing how big they are getting and comparing how big they are in relation to siblings and parents.

- Encourage children to use informal units of measure such as footsteps or blocks. Allow them to choose big or little steps, walking fast and slow, or counting only the steps made with the right or left foot. Counting in different ways while walking the same route (such as to school each day) encourages children to think about the importance of units to accurate measurement.

- Many daily activities involve measurement: cooking, gardening, grocery shopping, and repairing things around the house. Families can talk with children about what they are doing and what tools they are using to accomplish a task. For

Keeping track of children's height helps them see growth over time.

example: "The cake needs three teaspoons of vanilla." "How many cups of sugar do we need?"

- If possible, have children help with measurement chores by holding the ruler or filling the cup.

- Although parents need not attempt to teach young children conventional concepts of time, it is important for them to include language about time in their daily conversations and to highlight time concepts children can understand, such as the sequence of daily events or using paper links to count down the days to a special event. These early experiences help build the foundation for later concept development.

  - Use math vocabulary such as *about the same*, *near*, *approximately*, *more than*, and *fewer than*.

  - Help children to learn that some activities take longer than others: "Does it take longer to drive to school or to the grocery store? What do you think?"

  - Sing the ABCs or "Twinkle, Twinkle, Little Star" while brushing teeth and washing hands.

  - Use language in conversations that refers to time or sequences such as *before bed*, *after dinner*, or *"After school we'll go to the post office, then to the store, and then we'll go home."*

  - Provide toys during bath time that can be filled and emptied and come in different sizes, such as nesting cups, small water bottles, and plastic ladles.

It is important for teachers to emphasize that it is the language used during daily experiences that will help children learn concepts. By understanding more about what children know and are able to understand and what opportunities present themselves on a daily basis to talk about measurement concepts, family members will feel more confident in making math part of their regular interactions. In the course of a day, many activities will suggest themselves, and children will obtain practice with measurement concepts. When talking with family members before or after school each day, remember to highlight experiences their child may have had with measurement concepts and suggest something they can do on the way home, during dinner, or before bed that will reinforce the concept.

◇ Documenting and Assessing Children's Learning

Assessing emergent concepts of measurement will be a continuous activity done on an individual and group basis using the following tools and techniques (see the assessment tear-out sheets on pages 134 and 135):

- Observations of children's problem solving and conversations

- Small and large group discussions with students as they work individually and in groups

- Flexible interviews with students

- Portfolios of children's work collected throughout the year

- Children's self-evaluations, drawings, and dictated stories about measurement concepts

- Children's math journals

Children's growth in knowledge of emergent measurement concepts should be used to help plan the curriculum on the basis of their current understandings and the goals for the year. Teachers may create meaningful opportunities for children to demonstrate their understanding of measurement and how some things change in size over time (e.g., children, plants), while others remain the same (e.g., tables, toys). These experiences should be meaningful and relevant to children. For example, in a classroom where several children are expecting or recently welcomed new siblings into the family, they may be very aware of the differences in size between the infants and themselves. For children who have older siblings, they may be interested in why shoes that no longer fit an older child are handed down and the perfect size for the younger child. Documenting children's experiences, thoughts, and understanding of measurement concepts can be done through math journals, photos or drawings, and graphs. Chapters 1, 9, and 10 have many examples of ways that teachers can document and assess children's learning.

FOR THE CHILDREN

According to the *Principles and Standards for School Mathematics* (NCTM, 2000) and the National Research Council (NRC, 2010), young children begin to develop an understanding of attributes by looking at, touching, or directly comparing objects. They can identify which of two objects is heavier by lifting them or can compare their shoe sizes by putting them side by side. Accurate comparisons require the understanding of more complex measurement concepts, such as lining up the endpoints of two objects before comparing them. This idea will not be immediately obvious to children. They may also believe that rotating an object to a new orientation may change its length or width. But emergent experiences with measurement build to more formal understanding of complex measurement skills in the early elementary school years.

◇ Measuring

◆ Organize materials in the classroom by differences in size. For example, place crayons in small containers, markers in a slightly taller container, and colored pencils in the tallest container. Hang measuring cups and spoons or pretend pots and pans in the dramatic play area by size, providing the outlines of the materials to support children as they put them away. Organize the block shelf so that the smallest blocks are stored on the left, medium blocks in the middle, and longest blocks on the right. As children return materials to where they belong, this organization will expose them to concepts of measurement and seriation.

◆ Provide art materials that encourage children to explore measurement. Seriation concepts may be supported here by creating different shades of paint by adding one, two, or three pumps of white paint to one color. Have the children help you measure the white paint that goes into each color and then mix to make a new shade. Sample paint strips from a home repair store that include four to six variations of a color can be cut up and reorganized by children. Provide collage materials that come in different sizes, so teachers can ask questions about measurement as children create their artwork.

◆ Provide a large mural-sized piece of chart paper and many different types and sizes of construction paper or recycled paper shapes. Have children work together to fill the space, making sure that shapes do not overlap but also that there is no space between the shapes. This encourages children to consider the concept of area and to think about the size of shapes that will be needed to fill certain spaces.

Math manipulatives assist children in solving measurement problems.

◆ Use a balance scale to take attendance in the morning. Boys and girls may be represented by different-colored cubes or counting bears. When each child arrives in the morning, they place one cube in either the "boy" or "girl" side of the scale. Follow up by looking at the scale and determining whether there are more boys or girls present. Verify by counting the cubes in each side of the scale.

◆ Work with children to put links together in different lengths (from 2 to 10 links long). Compare the lengths of the link strands and discuss which are longer, shorter, or the same. Provide materials for children to compare to the lengths, such as a marker, a unit block, a puzzle board, or a book. Ask children to choose one of the link strands and then pick one of the materials they think has the same length as the strand. If children have difficulty choosing objects that are similar in length, model for them using the strand and lining it up against an object. Ask questions like, "Are my links too long for this block?" "Do I need a longer strand of links for this book?"

◆ Place standard units for measuring length, such as inch cubes and tape measures, in areas of the classroom that will encourage children to use them in meaningful ways, such as determining which block tower is higher or measuring the different lengths of play dough snakes. It is important for children to observe standard units being used appropriately and to hear the language modeled for them. Younger children may not always use standard units correctly, such as leaving spaces between units. The teacher can help, but facility with standard units will come with time.

◆ Create a matching game with cards that have "baby" and "mommy" animals on them (small and large). Play a memory or matching game with children, modeling measurement language and asking questions about how the animals differ.

◆ Plan a cooking project with the children based on their interests. Make a chart with the number of standard units of each ingredient that will be needed. Use pictorial representations as well. Assemble the standard units and have the children assist in measuring and combining the ingredients.

◆ Read *Is it larger? Is it smaller?* by Tana Hoban. This book has no words, so it is appropriate for all ages and abilities. Emphasize the language used in the story, such as *larger, smaller, biggest,* and *middle-sized.* Encourage children to compare

Capacity and volume are explored as children use containers of various sizes at the sand table.

objects by different attributes. Encourage children to find things in the classroom that are similar yet different in size—chart their answers or ask the children to draw pictures.

◆ Read *The Very Hungry Caterpillar* by Eric Carle. The "tiny and very hungry caterpillar" eats his way through the days, in the process of becoming a "beautiful butterfly." Children may slowly get the names of the days of the week in order, but more importantly they will see and remember the sequencing of events. Teachers can create sequencing cards with the different foods the caterpillar eats, and children can put them in order. The children may notice that as he goes through the week, how much he eats correlates with how big he gets.

◆ Place containers of various sizes in the sand and water tables. Let children experiment freely with filling and emptying containers and observe their behaviors. Model measurement behavior and language, such as "I want to fill up this big bucket. Which cup should I use for that? The big one or the little one?" Count as you fill the bucket. Then empty the bucket and ask a child to use a different cup to fill the bucket. Count together as you fill it up. Changing materials in the sand and water tables can lead to new experiences with volume and measurement. Adding water to sand makes it feel heavier; a cup with shaving cream is very light; red water takes up just as much space as green water. Remember that food is not an acceptable substitute for sand, because many children in our country come from homes where there is not enough food. Home repair or art supply stores will often donate materials that are interesting for children to play with.

◆ Place containers of various sizes at the sand table or use large containers filled with packing peanuts, shaving cream, or potting soil. Allow children to experiment freely with filling and refilling containers. Then pose questions for them to answer as previously suggested.

◆   Introduce a weighing station during a large group time. Using both familiar and unfamiliar materials, demonstrate for children how to compare the weights of objects by carefully using a balance scale. Items should vary by size and weight and include small and heavy (e.g., marbles, stones, or paperweights) and larger but light objects (e.g., balloons, foam blocks, or large pine cones). Ask the children which of two objects will be heavier, and demonstrate putting one item in each side. Use vocabulary such as *heavier* and *lighter* or *bigger* and *smaller*. Make the balance scales and objects available during center time. Charting results allows you to revisit the activity and results with children. This can be done by providing pictures of the materials and pockets where children can place the pictures. One side of the chart is labeled "heavier" and the other is labeled "lighter." After using the scale to test, children place pictures of the objects in pockets under the correct labels.

◆   Keeping track of time is difficult for young children, but placing a daily schedule in the room that is accessible to children allows you to refer to it frequently and remind children of the sequence of the day. The schedule should include pictures of the children during the different parts of the day, and it may include the time, or a clock with the time at which each part of the day occurs. For young children still learning the daily sequence, the teacher may want to move a symbol or a clothespin along the schedule at each part of the day and emphasize what has been done, what is happening right now, and what will happen next.

◆   There should be living things in the classroom for children to care for. Both animals and plants naturally provide many measurement activities associated with their care and feeding. For animals, children may be interested in measuring how much food and water the animals need each day, which can be done by tracking the level of water in the water bottle or by keeping track of how much goes into the food and water dishes each day. Children may measure the required amount of food in tablespoons or cups for each animal each day.

◆   Children are also very interested in plants and their growth and could also keep track of how much water the plants need and observe and document their growth and changes over time. Planting seeds provides opportunities for children to sort

Measuring plants on a regular basis helps children observe growth over time.

seeds by size, predict how tall plants of different sizes will grow, and create a chart that shows how much food, water, and sunlight each type of plant will need. As the plants grow, younger children may draw pictures to indicate the changes; older children will want to keep a record of the plants' growth over time in their math journals. Teachers will find more activities and suggested lessons on NCTM's Illuminations Web site (http://illuminations.nctm.org).

◇ Extending and Expanding to the Primary Grades

For Grade 1

Measurement is not considered a curriculum focal point for grade 1 (NCTM, 2006). It is connected to the primary focal points, however, in that children strengthen their sense of number by solving problems involving measurements and data. Representing measurements and discrete data in picture and bar graphs involves counting and comparisons. The related expectation for measurement in grade 1 is to recognize the attributes of length, volume, weight, area, and time. (Time is not identified as a focal point or connection for grade 1.)

For Grade 2

According to the curriculum focal points for grade 2, children develop an understanding of linear measurement and facility in measuring lengths. They understand the need for standard units of measure (centimeter or inch). Related expectations for grade 2 include the following:

- Recognize the attributes of length, volume, weight, and area.

- Understand how to measure using standard and nonstandard units.

- Select an appropriate unit and tool for the attribute being measured.

- Measure with multiple copies of units of the same size, such as paper clips laid end to end.

- Use repetition of a single unit to measure something larger than the unit—for instance, measuring the length of a room with a single meterstick.

- Use tools to measure.

- Develop common referents for measure to make comparisons and estimates.

For Grade 3

Measurement is not considered to be a curriculum focal point for grade 3. It is connected to the focal points as children in grade 3 confront problems in linear measurement that call for more precision than the whole unit used in grade 2. They form an understanding of perimeter as a measurable attribute and select appropriate units, strategies, and tools to solve problems involving perimeter.

Related expectations for grade 3 include these:

- Understand such attributes as length, area, weight (identified for grades 1 and 2), volume, and size of angle and select the appropriate type of unit for measuring each attribute.

- Carry out simple unit conversions, such as from centimeters to meters, within a system of measurement.

- Explore what happens to measurements of a two-dimensional shape (such as its perimeter and area) when the shape is changed in some way.

- Develop strategies for estimating the perimeters, areas, and volumes of irregular shapes.

- Select and apply appropriate standard units and tools to measure length, area, volume, weight, time, temperature, and the size of angles. (Measuring time and temperature is not identified as a focal point or connection.)

- Select and use benchmarks to estimate measurements.

Children in the early primary grades can do the following:

- Use their new vocabulary and knowledge of standard measures to understand the world. Introduce a unit on measurement by reading the poem "Take a Number" by Mary O'Neill, in *Marvelous Math: A Book of Poems*. This poem asks children to visualize a world without mathematics: no rulers or scales, inches or feet, prices or weights, days or nights—"Wouldn't it be awful to live like that?" Ask children to write a story about a world without math. Or, make a chart of all the things in the world that are related to math. The chart may be done over time with one or two words added each day.

- Build a larger and more complex vocabulary pertaining to measurement concepts. Make a word wall of all the things in the world that are related to math. You might want to list words in categories such as length, volume, weight, area, and time. Another wall can list tools of measurement such as rulers, scales of various types, yardsticks, and measuring cups.

- Understand units of measurement that are different from our own. Read *How Tall, How Short, How Faraway* by David A. Adler. Teachers can use that book in the following ways:

  - Help children to figure out their height using the units of measure of ancient Egypt—digits, palms, spans, and cubits. The book illustrates each unit. Compare children's heights.

  - Have children measure the length of the hall or the classroom using paces (measures used in ancient Rome). Compare answers. Then try another unit of measurement.

  - Allow children to work in small groups to plan and/or build a small town or pyramid, using the ancient measurement units. Children may draw a town, designating streets and buildings by size and distance. Or, they may choose to build a replica of an ancient Egyptian structure, using measurement from that time to plan.

- Understand that math problems can be difficult, but enjoy the challenge of solving math problems. Read *Math Curse* by Jon Scieszka and Lane Smith and discuss with older children just how many math problems there could be if they "think of almost everything as a math problem."

- Use *Anno's Math Games* by Mitsumasa Anno to find the answers to a multitude of math problems through a game format. Parents will also enjoy working with their children using this book or trying it for themselves.

- Use centimeter cubes. The more students work with the cubes as a standardized measure, the more easily they will recognize 1 centimeter as a length of space from the start of the cube to the end of the cube and not just a number on a ruler. Counting the number of cubes in an object's length can help students better visualize the differences in lengths among objects.

The teacher may also:

◆ Assist children in making their own ruler. They may call the unit of measure by whatever name they chose, but must make sure each unit is identical. Then challenge them to find objects that represent approximately each length on the ruler. Compare the lengths of objects according to individual rulers and encourage children to convert one another's measurements. For example, one child measures a book as five "moppets" long, while the same book is measured as twelve "cookies" long by another child's "ruler." The discussions that arise from these experiences will challenge children to think more critically about the importance of measurement concepts.

◆ Read *How Much Is a Million?* by David M. Schwartz. This book, with its charming illustrations, allows children to see the vastness of numbers such as a million or a billion. Of course, children will never be able to count that high, but the book provides some amusing concrete examples, such as "If a goldfish bowl were big enough for a million goldfish . . . it would be large enough to hold a whale." The many, many little stars give children an opportunity to see just "how many" objects can be. Older children can certainly profit more directly from this book. Children may enjoy creating their own pictures or perhaps a class book.

◆ Read *Measuring Penny* by Loreen Leedy. In addition to conveying that math homework can be fun, children find out in just how many ways something can be measured. Lisa has a homework assignment to measure something in as many ways as she can. "Use your imagination" is the last instruction. Lisa chooses her Boston terrier, Penny. She covers all possible measurements including conventional (height and weight) and unconventional ("How much it costs to take care of her"). Children can choose something in the classroom or at home to measure in as many ways as possible. Be creative!

Thinking About Measurement in the Kitchen

You may not realize it, but many things you and your children do in the kitchen help them learn about math! Here are some ideas for helping your children learn while you get things done in the kitchen.

Measuring ingredients—When children help to measure ingredients, they learn about differences in sizes and amounts. They may not need to know which spoon is a tablespoon and which is a teaspoon, but they can find the "biggest" or "smallest" one and help you count how many you need. They learn that the numbers on measurement tools have meaning.

Time—Children can keep track of the time it takes for certain things to cook or bake. If you need to boil water, use a stop watch to measure how long it takes. Or, use the microwave timer or a plastic hourglass to keep track of how much time something has left to bake. Time is a difficult concept for children to learn, but using it in a meaningful way, helps them understand it in a hands-on way.

Talking about measurement—As you work in the kitchen, there are some things young children may not be able to do (for example, using sharp knives to cut vegetables), but you can still talk about what you are doing. Notice how the pieces get smaller as you continue to cut them, or how the water rises in the pot when you add the pasta.

Try This!

Help children measure the ingredients and add them to the bowl.

Ask children to describe how the ingredients change as you mix them.

Ask how many cookies you think you can make with the dough and figure out how much dough should be used for each cookie. Compare the sizes of the different cookies.

Ask your child to set an egg timer or microwave timer for one hour.

No Bake Granola Bars

1 cup powdered sugar

1 cup creamy peanut butter

1/3 cup milk

1 teaspoon vanilla extract

1 1/2 cups uncooked oatmeal

1 cup granola cereal

1 1/4 cups chocolate chips

Add sugar, peanut butter, milk and vanilla to bowl. Stir until smooth. Add oats, cereal, and chips. Mix until combined. Roll into small balls and place on lined cookie sheet. Chill in refrigerator for at least one hour or until firm. www.pbs.org/parents/earlymath

Safety first!
—Keep all cleaning supplies in a locked cabinet.
—Make sure sharp knives and electronic equipment are out of reach.
—Never leave your child alone in the kitchen while the stove is on.
—Enjoy this time with your children and remember to HAVE FUN!

Exploring Measurement in our Classroom!

Dear Families,

We have been talking a lot about measurement in our classroom and exploring many different ways to use measurement. We wanted to let you know how we learn about measurement as we play each day.

Block Area

When we play with blocks, we learn about length, width, height, and area. These are big words for preschoolers, but we are learning about them as we make roads, build towers, and create different spaces for block people and animals to live in. We are always wondering who has the tallest tower, or which row of blocks is longer. We learn about area when we create a shape with the blocks and then fill it in with other blocks. This is something that will help us when we get to high school geometry class!

Sand and Water

This is one of our favorite learning areas. We use measuring cups and spoons to fill and empty different-sized bottles and buckets. This helps us learn about volume. Playing with sand and water lets us begin to understand differences in amount and how different kinds of spaces get filled up.

Small Toy Area

Lots of toys in this area teach us about measurement. Inch cubes, links, or small blocks can be used to measure the lengths and heights of different objects. Pegs and pegboards let us think about differences in height as we stack different colors on top of one another. Geoboards help us think about how to make shapes bigger or smaller by moving the rubber bands. We also love puzzles, which help us think about area and filling in different types of spaces.

These are just a few of our learning areas, but we are learning about measurement in all areas of our classroom! Here are some things you can do at home to keep us thinking about measurement:

- Play games with cars or balls to see who can get theirs to go the furthest, or which one can roll theirs the closest to a certain object.
- Play *Mother May I?* The leader stands on one side of the room or yard and the rest of the family stands on the other. Each person asks the leader if they may take a certain number of small, medium, or big steps toward the leader.
- Turn bath time into measurement time by giving children different sized buckets, cups, or bottles to fill and empty.
- Allow children to help organize the kitchen by sorting plates by size or matching pots and lids or plastic containers with the correct lids.

Assessing Children's Math Skills—Measurement

What to observe

Children working in the math or manipulative center, using materials that encourage measurement or comparison of length, such as links, inch cubes, pegs and peg boards, and so on

Children at the sand and water tables. Materials in these learning areas such as measuring cups and spoons and different-sized containers encourage thinking about measurement of volume

Play in the block area. Children often compare differences in the lengths and heights of their structures. They also often use measuring tapes in their first attempts at using standardized measurement tools

Outdoor play. Children explore measurement concepts such as distance, speed, and time and also often have opportunities to explore weight and volume in the sand area or by filling up buckets with different found materials

Activities—for individual or group assessment

Present problems that require measurement to solve (e.g., how many inch cubes it takes to fill up a given space, or making table cloths to cover different-sized tables)

Use and encourage children to use measurement language when comparing size, weight, volume, and so on

Ask children to organize materials by a measurement attribute (e.g., shortest to tallest, or lightest to heaviest)

Use different materials to measure the same objects (e.g., use inch cubes, links, and unit blocks to measure how long each child's sneaker is, then compare differences in quantities)

Follow-up questions

How can we figure out which one is longer, taller, heavier, bigger?

How do you know which one is longer, taller, heavier, bigger?

How are these things different/the same?

What happens if we use the small cups instead of the medium cups to fill up the big container? Will we use more small cups than medium cups or fewer?

How many more would I need to make mine the same size as yours?

Strategies

Uses nonstandard materials to estimate length, width, or height

Uses same unit of measurement (whether standard or nonstandard)

Compares two or more objects by using a common base (e.g., comparing two lengths of links, makes sure both start at the same spot)

Uses trial and error to solve measurement problems

Uses knowledge of measurement attributes to solve problems (e.g., needs to make structure a little bit taller, so chooses a small block to place on top)

Individual Evaluation: Assessing Children's Math Skills—Measurement

Date:

Child:

Area of classroom or activity:

Activity used:

Observation notes

Follow-up questions and responses:

Quick summary—Child:
Notices large differences in size
Compares two or more objects using one or more measurement attributes
Accurately arranges objects in order of size or another measurable attribute
Solves problems using measurement
Uses standard or nonstandard measurement materials to compare differences in objects
Uses measurement language to describe differences in attributes
Understands that measurement units need to be the same
Makes estimates based on prior knowledge of measurement attributes

Data Description, Organization, Representation, and Analysis

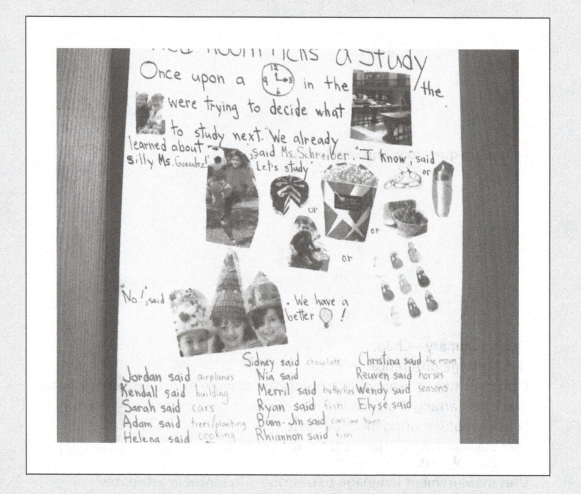

———————————————— FOR THE TEACHER ————————————————

◇ **What You'll Need to Know**

In order to answer questions that interest us, we often need to first collect and organize data. Although data analysis may sound complicated and abstract, in the early years it simply requires that children observe and comment on phenomena, categorize and record by shared attributes, and evaluate the organization to come to conclusions or ask new questions. Clements and Sarama (2009) suggest that in the early years, "Curricula and teachers might focus on one big idea: Classifying, organizing, representing, and using information to ask and answer questions." This is done with the teacher's guidance and can be quite engaging for children when it revolves around topics that interest them.

Data analysis and probability are not considered curriculum focal points for prekindergarten or kindergarten (NCTM, 2006). Data analysis is connected to the focal points, however, in that children use attributes to sort, describe, or compare objects as they work to solve problems. The related expectation for prekindergarten is to sort and classify objects according to their attributes and organize data about the objects. Related expectations for kindergarten children include the following:

- Posing questions and gathering data about themselves and their surroundings

- Sorting and classifying objects according to their attributes, and organizing data about the objects

- Describing parts of the data and the set of data as a whole to determine what the data show

For young children to successfully meet the requirements of mathematics standards in the elementary and upper school years, they will need to know how to collect, describe, organize, represent, and analyze their findings. In the process of doing so, they are becoming familiar with the ideas of statistics and probability. Whitin and Whitin (2003) explain how their kindergarten children were familiar with, and excited about, data collection. In addition to daily lunch graphs, they had experiences with surveys, lists, and bar graphs. They voted for names of class pets, counted birds at the bird feeder, and represented statistics such as birthdays or favorite foods. Clements (1999b) describes how very young children like working with substantial mathematics ideas. The inner-city minority children he studied were self-motivated to investigate what numbers mean and how they work, leading Clements to conclude that there may be no better time to introduce substantial mathematical concepts such as data description, organization, representation, and analysis.

For example, a group of 3- and 4-year-olds from New York City was interested in transportation and the different ways each child traveled to school each day. Some children walked, some took the subway, some rode in cars, and others took the bus. Responding to their interests, the teachers asked the children one morning how they each traveled to school. Using a chart, she divided it into four sections and used tally marks for each child's method of transportation. One child presented a problem because some days he took the subway and other days he took a bus. The teacher suggested he could go in the category that he used the most. So, they counted the days and compared to determine which one he used more. After all children responded, some of the older children were able to tell from looking at the tally marks which mode was most frequent, but the teacher decided to use vehicle counters to create a visual graph. She asked children to help her organize the data with the vehicle counters and used counting bears to represent children who walked. After counting the right number for each section, the teacher lined them up so children could compare the groups. The conversation about transportation led children to further exploration in various learning areas of the classroom. As can be seen here, young children's firsthand experiences with their here-and-now world naturally lead to using ideas of data description, organization, representation, and analysis.

Children do not automatically come to the preschool with the ability to discuss what is largest or tallest, to talk about their findings, or to graph them. Early experiences with observing and commenting on attributes and organizing and describing data must be modeled first by teachers, and children must be guided to notice attributes, comment on them, and organize and describe them. Teachers may suggest to children that they might want to remember what they said at a later time and wonder out loud how children might do that. Very often, scientific explorations lend themselves to this kind of data analysis. Children can observe, comment on, and document data regarding nature, simple experiments, and scientific questions.

◇ **Key Concepts**

- The study of statistics involves collecting, organizing, and sorting data.

- Concepts of labeling and scaling are crucial to data representation.

- Data can be described through graphs, tables, and lists.

- The process of analyzing and interpreting data involves recognizing patterns or trends and gaining information from graphs.

- In the process of organizing data, children make inferences or predictions and have initial experiences with probability.

◇ **Goals and Objectives**

- Children will observe and comment on attributes and phenomena.

- Children will collect, organize, and sort data.

- Children will begin to label information collected and develop an understanding of scale.

- Children will organize data through pictures, graphs, tables, lists, and so on.

- Children will gain meaning from graphs, tables, and lists by being able to find more/less; most/least; tallest/lowest; none, same, all; longest/shortest; fewer, least, all; higher/taller.

◇ **What You'll Need**

Curcio, F. R. (2010). *Developing Graph Comprehension.* This book, published by NCTM, provides resources for using data with children in a way that is relevant and interesting. It guides teachers with activities for recording and analyzing data from various sources, including the Internet, newspapers, and magazines.

Lee, M., & Miller, M. (1999). *Great Graphing.* This book, which offers 60 ideas for graphing with children in grades 1–4, can also spur preschool teachers' ideas for creating graphs with younger children.

Polonsky, L. (Ed.). (2000). *Math for the Very Young: A Handbook of Activities for Parents and Teachers.* Written by teachers involved with the University of Chicago School Mathematics Project, this guide offers teachers a comprehensive collection of activities for teaching all areas of math to young children.

Children's Books

Almost all of the children's math books cited in this text may be used for creating classification schemes and graphing. For example, the following books lend themselves to graphic representations:

Crews, D. (1995). *Ten Black Dots.*

Falwell, C. (1993). *Feast for 10.*

Hutchins, P. (1986). *The Doorbell Rang.*

Merriam, E. (1996). *12 Ways to Get to 11.*

Reid, M. (1990). *The Button Box.*

Other good books include these two:

deRubertis, B. (1999). *A Collection for Kate.*

Keenan, S., & Girouard, P. (1997). *More or Less a Mess.*

 ## The Home–School Connection

Families can participate in data collection in many ways. The simplest way is to conduct surveys occasionally, where children are responsible for going home and collecting data to bring back to school. Engaging families in this process shows them that asking and answering simple questions can be used as a foundation for teaching many mathematical concepts. Following children's interests, teachers may send them home with a question. For example, at the beginning of the school year, much of the daily conversation revolved around families in the children's homes. During one discussion with a small group, the children became interested in discussing who ate dinner with them at home. As a result, each child went home with a question, "Who eats dinner with you?" Reporting back, children drew pictures of their families and created a graph depending on how many people ate dinner together each night.

Other questions will arise naturally throughout the year, and some may be prompted by the teacher when she recognizes ideas that interest children. Making this informal data collection a regular part of the curriculum validates children's lives outside of school, engages families in the learning process, and creates a true sense of community. Remember to send home results of surveys, explaining them to families and sharing with them how interested the class is in documenting their life experiences at home and at school.

In addition to surveys, teachers can involve families in these other ways:

- When important graphs are constructed, take digital photos of them to e-mail or print out and send home to families. Explain the concept being graphed, how children and teachers constructed the graph, and how to discuss the graph with children.

- Use newsletters to inform parents about children's learning to sort, organize, represent, and analyze data. Let families know that much of young children's learning occurs through spontaneous events. Children learn as they explore their world. But informal learning does not mean unplanned learning. Parents can plan activities such as these:

  - Point out circle or bar graphs in grocery or other stores, on signs, or in a newspaper or magazine.

(a)

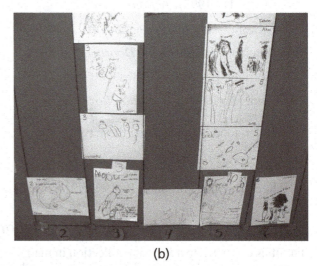

(b)

Children collect and represent data about who eats dinner together each night.

- Help children collect and organize things in the home environment. Create and organize shopping lists by the areas of the grocery store or keep track of family data such as the types of mail that arrive each day, the number of people at the dinner table each night, or the time it takes to get to school each day.

- Provide access to books and ideas that extend children's ideas of mathematics. A book you could recommend is *Family Math* by Jean Kerr Stenmark, Virginia Thompson, and Ruth Cossey.

◇ Documenting and Assessing Children's Learning

The point of collecting and representing information through graphs is to familiarize children with the fact that they can organize and then gain meaning from pictorial descriptions of the things they find through explorations of their world.

Classroom Observations

As children work in various learning areas throughout the classroom, pay attention to their play and the materials they use that may encourage classification, organization, or data analysis. Sorting games, puzzles, many different types of manipulatives, and science activities will all require children to notice attributes and make decisions based on those attributes. Very young children may build with only one type of block or stack all pegs of one color together. This is the evidence of the earliest stages of data collection and analysis, as children begin to organize their world based on attributes. Because children at this age may not be able to verbalize their organizational scheme, it is important to model the language, "Oh, I see you've put all of the squares in this bowl and all of the triangles in this other bowl. This is a rectangle—does it go in one of these bowls?" As children grow, they will be able to organize on more sophisticated levels, such as the child who sorted plastic animals into groups of herbivores and carnivores. This ability represents the child's ability to think about attributes that are not immediately present.

Flexible Interviews

Flexible interviews with individual children uncover children's abilities to notice similarities and differences among attributes as well as their thinking about graphs and data organization.

Ask children to organize materials or information by a rule they create, or organize data and ask younger children to tell you what the rule is. Older children can work together to organize data by a rule and then ask others to try and guess what the rule is. Ask children to talk to you about a familiar graph, chart, or pictorial description of findings. First, ask an open-ended question such as "What can you tell me about this?" Probe further, asking "What else do you know about this?" or "What do we call this?" Record the child's answers.

Finish the interview by asking the child questions about the meaning of the graph. For example, if the graph depicts the number of children who have pets, ask if more children have pets or if more do not; if the graph depicts children's favorite foods, ask which food is the favorite, the next best, and so on. Remember that young children are likely unable to think about the graph as a whole and might only focus on the individual data (Clements & Sarama, 2009), such as where they or their friends are individually represented on the graph (e.g., "That's my name, I liked the red apples the best.").

From structured interviews you will be able to gain an understanding of each child's thinking about data analysis. This will help you plan the next graphing experience in ways that will match children's existing ideas and extend or clarify them.

—————————— FOR THE CHILDREN ——————————

◇ Collecting and Analyzing Data

1. Children Will Observe and Comment on Attributes and Phenomena

Before children can collect and organize data, they must learn to identify attributes and comment on naturally occurring phenomena. This includes simple observations such as "I have two brothers" or "We are wearing the same colored shirt today." These simple observations lead children to questions about the world that can be answered by collecting, organizing, and analyzing data.

◆ Provide children with many opportunities to observe and describe naturally occurring phenomena. This includes nature walks, simple science experiments, and similarities or differences among classmates.

◆ Model observation language by calling attention to similarities or differences among attributes of materials children are playing with. Call attention to colors, sizes, patterns, and interesting phenomena such as the way certain paint colors can be mixed together to create a new color, or how it seems to get darker earlier each day. As you model observation skills for children, they will become more observant and want to share with you and the class the interesting things in their environment that they take notice of.

2. Children Will Collect, Organize, and Sort Data

The ability to collect, organize, and sort data is an important underpinning for algebra and reasoning skills, as well as the foundation for data description and analysis. Children begin early to form groups. First, children pick things from a group of objects on the basis of one characteristic (Copley, 2000): "This is round." Often, however, children just beginning the process of classification cannot tell you why they make the sets they do, or they will say something like "They're all my favorite." Next, children sort entire collections of objects by a single attribute, placing all the round, or red, or fuzzy objects together. At the third level, which may not occur until kindergarten, children sort objects or events on the basis of two or more characteristics: "All of these are round and red." During this process, children also learn to identify missing attributes by telling you why objects do or do not belong to a given group.

◆ Children are natural collectors. They pick up rocks, leaves, seeds—not just to handle but also to collect. To foster children's collecting, give each child a small paper bag before going on a walk around the block. One walk could be for children to collect leaves in the bag. Back in the classroom, children may want to sort their leaves by size or color. Once this is decided, teachers can help children record the number of leaves they have in each size or color. Other trips can be taken to collect different colors, sizes, or types of stones, acorns, or pine cones.

◆ Create a shelf or corner of the room for play-yard supplies. On the shelf, include small cardboard boxes or paper bags to be used for collecting when outside and several clear plastic containers for additional collections.

◆ To foster children's collecting, ask them why they made the collections they did, or if the objects could be sorted in another way. If a child sorted a collection based on size or shape, challenge her to reorganize it based on color or the number of points on each leaf.

◆ Read *A Collection for Kate* by Barbara deRubertis, a book about children bringing their collections to school. At school, the collections can be categorized and subcategories counted. You might follow the story and ask children about their collections or start a class collection.

◆ Add materials to the math area that support classification. Provide plastic bowls of different colors for sorting items, or a cupcake pan or egg carton with spots labeled for different materials. Empty cupcake pans with small, precut circles of paper may be labeled by children to fit their own classification rules. There are many materials made to support thinking about classification, but natural materials work just as well, along with materials that can be collected, such as buttons, keys, or bottle caps.

◆ Offer children a "discovery box." In it, collect all types of things—discarded keys, locks, or key chains; large marbles; discarded pens; childproof kitchen tools such as a nutcracker, a small sieve, or a tea ball; and odds and ends from your own junk drawer. Make sure that there are no duplicates for any of the items. First ask children to play with the materials; then you could ask them to do some of the following things:

  • Find two objects that are the same in some way. One child picked out a plastic fork and a plastic key chain, saying they were the same because they were both made of plastic; another child picked out a brownish acorn and a piece of wood, saying they were the same color.

  • Pick out an item that is like the thing the teacher has picked out.

  • Sort the items into things that are the same or different. Have children discuss why and how they made their categories. As children do so, record their responses.

Repeat the experience several times during the year. You should see children moving from arbitrary collections to collections based on the attributes of the items in the box.

3. Children Will Begin to Label Information Collected and Develop an Understanding of Scale

"All these are brown rocks," said 4-year-old Misha, showing his teacher a box of rocks he had collected. "I need a label that says *Brown Rocks*." The teacher asked him to think about how the word *brown* starts, saying, "Listen: *brown*—What letter should I write first?" Misha responded saying, "It's the /b/ sound, but I don't know how to write the rest of it." Together they wrote a label for the box and placed it on the science table.

◆ Let children see you writing labels and titles on charts and graphs:

- As you write, say the word and say each letter.

- Read the labels or titles to the children and ask them to read these back to you.

- Print in the classroom should be placed intentionally, in ways that serve a purpose, such as where to find materials and then return them when you are done, a sign over the sink that shows how to wash your hands, and a chart that shows who is present and absent today. Labeling chairs with the word *chair* does not help children understand the purpose of print, which is to convey meaning or to communicate with others.

◆ Encourage children to take pictures from different angles of their structures in the block area. When looking at the pictures and comparing them to the actual structures, children will notice difference in size and perspective and begin to think about the concept of scale. Older children may be able to represent simple structures on paper, recognizing that the drawing does not need to be true to size.

◆ When younger children play with dolls and doll houses, they are developing an understanding of scale: They recognize that they do not sit on the doll-house chairs because they are too small. But they do know that the dolls fit on the chairs, correctly matching the doll and toy chair. Teachers can ask questions or make comments that challenge children's perspectives and cause them to think about scale. Their drawings of families will eventually move from circles and legs, to smaller circles and legs for children and bigger circles and legs for adults, to stick figures of relatively accurate sizes. Notice when children accurately represent family members in the smaller scale and ask them to draw a tree or a flower to see if they continue.

4. Children Will Organize Data Through Graphs, Tables, Lists, and So On

As children become more proficient at collecting and organizing data, they will learn to represent it in various ways. But understanding requires repeated exposure to different methods, such as tallies or numbers to represent their experience. They need to observe their experiences being represented in lines or numbers. While using tallies, introduce children to the idea of using columns and rows. Use tallies to keep track of how many times a child can jump rope on one foot and on two feet. Make tallies or use numbers in rows and columns:

One Foot	Two Feet
111111	1111111111

Stages in making and understanding graphs have been identified (Charlesworth & Radeloff, 1978). During the first stage of graph making, children use either themselves or real objects to make graphs, but graph only two variables or objects. Next, more than two items are considered, and a more permanent record is constructed. In the third stage of graphing, children can use symbols, such as check marks or squares of paper, to chart their findings.

◆ Construct graphs. Graphing with young children should be as concrete as possible. Often teachers begin graphing experiences using the children themselves to make the graph. Make graphs of children by having them stand in one of two lines to find out things such as the following:

- How many children came to school on the bus today? How many children walked? Count the children in each line.

- Which children eat lunches brought from home and which eat lunches made at school?

- How many children have siblings and how many do not?

- How many boys and how many girls are in the group?

- Which children like apples and which prefer pears?

Be sure to count the children in each group, record the count on a chart, and reach conclusions about how many children were in each line and which line had the most children, the least children, or even no children. Younger children may need actual pictures of objects; older children will be able to interpret tally marks.

Once children are used to counting themselves and seeing the information being written and then read back to them, begin creating graphs with unit blocks. Tape a child's name to the side of each block. Instead of standing in a line and being counted, each child places his or her block under the correct label. The blocks are counted, and the number in each stack recorded and discussed. You might use the blocks to chart and record the following:

- The number of children in school

- Children who have pets and those who do not

- Children wearing something red and those who are not wearing anything red

- Children who like fruit and those who do not

A group of 3-year-olds graphed their height, building with cardboard blocks to equal their height. The blocks were stacked in a row, and each child stood by his or her stack of blocks.

◆ Make floor graphs. Children can construct graphs using poster boards, a piece of flannel, or large construction paper placed on the floor. They can place small pictures, cutouts, and small photos of themselves; plastic/wooden animals, people, buildings, and cars; or other objects and items in rows to make graphs of the following:

- Farm and zoo animals, animals they know, and those they have never seen

- Whether they saw a square or a circle on their way to school

- The learning center they prefer to play in

- Yes or no answers to the questions "Do you have . . . ?" "Do you like . . . ?" "Have you been to . . . ?" or "Do you enjoy . . . ?"

◆ Use cash register tape for graphs:

- Measure the height of a bean plant each day, and record each day's growth on a piece of register tape.

- Chart and record each child's height and weight using cash register tape.

- Use register tape to chart and record the number of inches of rain or snow that falls in a given week.

- Chart and record the height of block buildings using register tape.

◆ Moving from the concrete to the abstract, you can construct graphs using paper and markers, pictures, colored paper squares, blocks, and other materials:

- Ask children to count the number of birds they see at the bird feeder at different points during the day. You might find bird pictures or stickers of birds common to the area and use these to make a pictorial graph of "Birds at the Feeder."

- Observe the number of cars passing by the center during a given time. Count the cars or trucks and, using pictures or stickers of vehicles, record your findings.

◆ First graphing experiences continue moving from the concrete to the abstract and involve only two categories.

Make a graphing tray. Cupcake pans lend themselves nicely to this, because they come in three rows of four, which allows for simple graphing. Provide children with small objects to sort to create a graph. You might give them a box of two types of animals (farm and zoo), a box of small cars and trucks, or a box of small plastic people and children. The point is to fill the three rows of cups with the different objects to create a graph. Then children count and compare the number of objects in each category.

◆ All graphing activities should stem from something of high interest to children. Teachers who base the curriculum on the resources found in the children's environment will find plenty of interesting things for children to graph. For instance:

- Children are interested in superheroes and cartoon characters. Surveying children for their favorites is fun and engaging.

- After a mother came to the class and played a violin, the children were taught to pick out a melody on the piano, and they listened to their favorite songs played on the violin and piano. To reach closure, the children graphed which music they liked best—violin or piano. The children asked the teacher for a third category, "Both Violin and Piano," because they "liked both of them." To make this graph, children colored in a square under the appropriate label.

- Children visiting a farm were impressed when the farmer said she measured her horse with her hands. Her horse was 16 hands high. Back in the classroom, children measured things in their room with their hands and made a graph of cutout hands.

- Children studying themselves created graphs of eye and hair color.

- One group of 5-year-olds, who were studying clothing, made graphs to represent the different ways their shoes closed. The graph titled "Shoes" included categories for *Tie Shoes*, *Velcro*, *Slip-Ons*, and *Buckle Shoes*.

Children document a measurement experience using their hands as the measurement instrument.

- Children who had visited a shoe store were given a foot measure to use in their classroom. The 3-year-olds enjoyed measuring their feet with and without shoes. After the play waned, the teacher asked them to measure their shoes. The lengths of children's shoes were recorded on a graph, and the children decided that most of them wore the same size shoes. The teacher sent home a survey asking family members to record their shoe sizes, and as the children brought the responses back, they continued to add to the graph.

- One teacher of 4-year-olds introduced children to concepts of story structure and genre. After reading several folktales—*Three Little Pigs*, *Little Red Riding Hood*, and *Three Billy Goats Gruff*—she asked children to talk about parts of the stories or characters that were the same or different. She created a Venn diagram, and children were able to visualize what the stories had in common.

    Another week, the teacher read a group of current stories. She then asked children to vote for their favorite current story and their favorite folktale. Recording their votes in a graph, the children compared stories they liked. Huber and Lenhoff (2006) suggest graphing experiences to underscore the mathematical connections between literature and real life. An important component for children is the interpretation of the information represented.

- When children studied the way their clothing was closed, they noted that some items were held together with ties and other items with zippers, buttons, or Velcro. A chart was made titled "Our Clothing," with the categories *Ties*, *Buttons*, *Zippers*, and *Velcro*.

    Then the children counted just the number of buttons on shirts, jeans, and sweaters and graphed their findings. They found that the majority of children had six buttons on their coats. The experiences of counting and graphing buttons—and shoe sizes, clothing, and so forth—serve as foundational knowledge for the learning of the meaning of *mode*, which will come later in children's lives.

Children can use Venn diagrams to record and reflect on similarities and differences among things.

Children vote for their favorite jack-o-lantern stencil.

- Votes need a way of being recorded. Children's preferences for any number of things or events can be recorded in a graph. The teacher for a group of 4-year-olds brought in a pumpkin to carve. The children could not decide what kind of face they wanted to carve on the pumpkin, so they voted. The teacher helped them make a chart with the five different jack-o-lantern stencils, and each child placed a cutout of a pumpkin on the chart above the stencil he or she chose.

◆ Introduce children to pie charts. Early experiences with pie charts expose children to the concepts of measurement and fractions. Although these charts are more abstract than comparing the height of lines in a line graph, pie charts can be used by older children and constructed from paper circles, paper plates, or tinfoil pans. The point is to divide the circle space in ways that represent children's ideas or specific categories. Begin with simple representations of only two things, such as boys and girls in the class, or choosing milk or juice for snack. With only two choices, it is clear that one is preferred more than another. To help children understand how the pie chart works, divide the circle into as many "pieces" as there are children in the class. As children vote, allow them to color in one section of the chart with the color that represents their choice.

◆ Encourage children to conduct surveys and chart the results in graph form. Providing clip boards and erasable graphs and prompting questions encourages children to survey the class and record the data.

- During a study of grocery stores, a group of 5-year-olds became interested in where foods came from. They interviewed the kitchen staff to find out where the food in the kitchen came from. They surveyed the class to find out where each family bought most of their food. But a few children were not content with the answer "grocery stores" or "markets"; they wanted to know where the food at the market came from. So they conducted another survey and asked family members to help identify where some of the foods in their homes came from. This provided satisfying results, as answers came back and children discovered that foods they ate came from around the state, from across the country, and from around the world.

- Another group surveyed adults working in the school to find out what their favorite foods were. The children also interviewed family members. With the teacher's help, children charted the favorite foods of adults. They then compared the adults' favorite foods to their own and made another graph that illustrated foods both adults and children liked.

5. Children Will Gain Meaning from Graphs, Tables, Lists, and So On

"What is this?" a visiting supervisor asked 3-year-old children as she pointed to a graph on the wall. "We ate baby cereal," said one child. Another child pointed to the pictures of children on the graph, where most were placed under the banana or the apple. She said, "We all like the fruit!" The supervisor saw that the children had tried two fruits and two vegetables, and the children had agreed that they preferred the fruit. There was one child who voted for sweet potatoes, and he chimed in, "Not me! I like this one," and pointed to his picture under the sweet potato.

The supervisor complimented the teacher, saying, "You know, I'm used to seeing graphs in preschools and asking children what they mean. And I'm also used to children saying 'I don't know,' which tells me the teacher made the graph with no input from the children. Your children, because it was an activity they were interested in and they actually participated in preparing the graph, knew exactly what it meant."

Although it is easy for teachers to make graphs, it is not easy for young children to understand them. Graphs incorporate several number skills and understandings. To understand graphs, children need some idea of the following concepts:

- One-to-one correspondence

- Counting

- Comparing more or less

- Numerals and their names

- The correspondence between numerals and quantity

◆   As the teacher of the 3-year-olds did with the cereal, you can make graphs meaningful for children of any age. Follow these guidelines:

- Make sure graphing stems from a real experience.

- Read the graph with individual children and ask questions like these:

Which has the most?	Which is longest?
Which has the least?	What is the same as?
Is there more or less?	What do some of the children like?
What is heavier/lighter?	Which is rough/smooth?

- Use words such as *none, all, some, most, least, a lot, longest, tallest, shortest,* and so on to describe the data. Use the number "0" to represent no children or no results for a particular category. It is important for children to connect the number "0" to its quantity just as we want them to connect other numbers with their quantities.

Children collect and represent data about their favorite type of apple.

- Refer to the information on the graph: "We voted for . . ." or "Do you remember which one most of the children wanted to . . .?" In addition to questioning, discuss the problem or the reason children made the graph and talk about what the graph means.

- Make the home–school connection by sending copies of graphs to parents with explanations of what the children did and what their graphs mean. Send home family graphs that they can complete together and that children can bring back to school to compare. Older children may be able to look at different graphs representing families and draw some conclusions, such as "Jeremy's family likes tomatoes the best, but my family likes carrots the best."

◇ Reflecting

In a way, creating and reading graphs give children a way to reflect and think about their experiences. By organizing information, graphs inform children of trends as well as central tendency. Obviously, it will be a long time before children need to understand trends and central tendency (mean and mode). Regardless, graphs introduce children to these concepts.

As children read graphs, ask them to reach conclusions: "What is our favorite story?" "What games do we like the best?" "Why do you think only two children voted for the scary jack-o-lantern?"

◇ Extending and Expanding to the Primary Grades

Data analysis and probability are not considered curriculum focal points for grade 1, grade 2, or grade 3.

For Grade 1 and Grade 2

Related expectations for grade 1 in data analysis include the following:

- Sorting and classifying objects according to their attributes and organizing data about the objects

- Representing data using concrete objects, pictures, and graphs

- Describing parts of the data and the set of data as a whole to determine what the data show

There are no related expectations for grade 2.

For Grade 3

For grade 3, data analysis is connected to the focal points. Addition, subtraction, multiplication, and division of whole numbers come into play as students construct and analyze frequency tables, bar graphs, picture graphs, and line plots and use them to solve problems. Related expectations for grade 3 in the area of data analysis and probability are as follows:

- Design investigations to address a question and consider how data-collection methods affect the nature of the data set.

- Collect data using observations, surveys, and experiments.

- Represent data using tables and graphs such as line plots, bar graphs, and line graphs.

- Describe the shape and important features of a set of data and compare related data sets.

- Compare different representations of the same data and evaluate how well each representation shows important aspects of the data.

- Propose and justify conclusions and predictions that are based on data and design studies to further investigate the conclusions or predictions. (Designing such studies is not identified as a focal point or connection.)

Graphing that begins during the early years lays the foundation for more complicated graphing in the primary grades. In the primary grades, children can do the following:

- Construct their own graphs using any number of variables represented by numbers displayed in columns and rows.

- Begin developing ideas of central tendency, finding the mean and mode on graphs.

- Start thinking about probability. Children might shake two-color chips in a shaker and then graph, perhaps using toothpicks or tallies, the number of times each color comes up. Using 10 counters, children can next count the number of times the blue sides were up and the red sides were up, practicing addition.

- Graph week- or month-long events, charting or graphing which month has the most birthdays, what time children go to bed and wake up, or how many holidays there are in each month or the entire year.

- Use larger numbers. Children might graph how many pieces of popcorn different cups or containers can hold or how many kernels are found in bags of different brands of popcorn after popping, or they could guess how many pieces of popcorn are on a paper plate, charting their names, guesses, and the exact popcorn count.

The fantastic thing about data collection and representation is that children can always make it personal and meaningful, investigating and communicating in an organized way about topics that are important to them. This organization allows them to ask and answer questions about their experiences both firsthand and vicariously, as in children's literature. As children are involved in data collection, graphing, and analysis, they learn many strategies for problem solving and how to communicate their answers to others. Graphing and data analysis offer many ways for children to document what they have learned through their investigations. They provide an important way to display and communicate the results of active experiences.

10

Learning to Problem-Solve

──────────────────── **FOR THE TEACHER** ────────────────────

◇ **What You'll Need to Know**

Young children, filled with curiosity, are natural problem solvers. From the moment of birth, children begin the process of observing, looking, and listening. In an attempt to make sense of the world in which they find themselves, children actively explore their world. They feel, put things in their mouths, take things apart, and pull, push, tear, pick up, and drop things—all to try to find out more about the nature of the things in their world. Persistence in problem solving and the ability to apply information from previous experiences to new situations, or in a new way, is the key to success in all areas of learning but is essential to success in mathematics. Problem solving is not a curriculum focal point for any of the grades, prekindergarten through grade 3. Rather, it is embedded in all of them.

Within the context of a high-quality early childhood classroom, children have time, freedom, and opportunity to extend and expand their natural problem-solving skills. Teachers model problem-solving sequences for children, focus on the strategy rather than the solution, and encourage children to be persistent and to try again after a failure. Through these experiences, children learn to ask questions, collect data, reflect, and solve real problems. As they do so, they develop the ability to identify and solve problems coming from daily life, as well as develop number and other mathematical knowledge and skills.

Children appear to come hard-wired to ask questions: "What's dis? Dat?" "How much money do you have?" "Why is there more here?" These first questions are sometimes asked to express wonder and surprise with the world (Piaget & Inhelder, 1969). Curious 4- and 5-year-olds continue to ask "Why?" Often, however, they really do want to know *why:* "Why are there three ducks?" They really want to know causal relations: "Why is it heavy?" "Why does she have more?" The role of the teacher is to model questions that will stretch children's thinking and understanding. As children build in the block area, rather than asking, "What did you make?" teachers focused on supporting problem solving will ask, "How did you get this block to balance here?" or "What might happen if you put this big block on top of the small ones?"

Because of the wide variety of math experiences children encounter each day (Seo & Ginsburg, 2004), teachers have many opportunities to support children's problem-solving skills. Larry Buschman (2003), an elementary school teacher, understands the importance of the teacher's role in problem solving: "One of the greatest challenges facing teachers of problem solving is to shift their focus away from what children cannot do and toward what children can do. Instead of pointing out children's errors and telling them how to fix their mistakes, we should focus on what children already know, then build on that knowledge." The box on page 158 suggests some ways for teachers to model questioning skills and focus on what children can do.

Problem solving begins with observation and asking questions. Children come to school with observation skills—notice toddlers pointing to every interesting thing they observe. But preschoolers must focus attention on using their senses to obtain information that will lead to questions and help them solve problems. Sometimes, teachers may ask children to focus on using one sense at a time—to really look, listen, or feel and touch. At other times, children might be asked to use all of their senses at once—to look, look again, listen, touch, and handle and feel.

Once children learn to critically observe and verbally express their observations, there must be some way for them to organize their findings through collections, displays, graphs, or the other methods described in Chapter 9. Children reflect on and think about their findings and ask questions about their discoveries. Teachers guide children as they make plans to find the answers to their questions.

Mathematical problem solving is central to learning mathematics. It is through problem solving—observing and collecting information, organizing the information, sensing a problem, posing questions, and reaching conclusions—that children have opportunities to apply their mathematical knowledge and skills. Whether children are asking questions, observing, finding out, or reaching conclusions, they will need to apply their knowledge and skills of counting, number operations, graphing, measuring, working with shapes, or beginning concepts of algebra.

◇ **Key Concepts**

- Problem solving begins by observing and commenting on phenomena.

- All the senses are used to collect information around the topic or area of interest. Vicarious information, books, CDs, and Web information can be used to extend and expand children's firsthand experiences.

- Information or data must be collected and organized in some representational way.

- Information collected—the data—is analyzed. The processes of reflection and sensing a problem and posing thoughtful questions lead to creating a plan to solve the problem.

- Reaching conclusions or asking new questions constitutes the final stage of problem solving.

- The problem-solving processes are embedded in all areas of mathematics: knowledge of numbers, counting, measuring, graphing, beginning algebra, and geometry.

◇ **Goals and Objectives**

Mathematical problem solving means that children will use mathematical concepts and skills to engage in a task for which the solution may not be immediately evident. This means children will use the knowledge they have and the processes of problem solving to develop new mathematical understandings.

Applying counting, algebra, geometry, measuring, and data organization to solving problems, the following goals and objectives will be achieved:

- Children will develop the ability to make careful observations and comment on phenomena.

- Children will begin to organize information in representational ways.

- Children will analyze data and ask new, related questions.

- Children will use data to reach conclusions.

- Children will gain skills in reflecting.

◇ **What You'll Need**

O'Connell, S. (2007). *Introduction to Problem Solving, Grades PreK–2*.

Lester, F. K., & Charles, R. I. (2003). *Teaching Mathematics Through Problem Solving: Pre-kindergarten–Grade 6*.

Buschman, L. (2003). *Share and Compare: A Teacher's Story About Helping Children Become Problem Solvers in Mathematics*. This book contains resources for teachers of children in kindergarten to grade 5, but the approaches to problem solving are appropriate for younger children. The author provides resources for communicating with parents about the importance of problem solving, as well as documentation of children's varying levels of problem-solving abilities.

National Council of Teachers of Mathematics (NCTM). (2000). *Principles and Standards for School Mathematics.* The Standards for PreK–2—specifically the standard for problem solving—will be useful to teachers. Teachers can access the information at the NCTM Web site (www.nctm.org/standards/content.aspx?id=26852).

U.S. Department of Education. (n.d.). *Let's Do Math.* This pamphlet provides ideas for parents and teachers to help children learn and enjoy math at a young age. It is available online at the Web site of the U.S. Department of Education (www.ed.gov/pubs/parents/LearnPtnrs/math.html).

Children's Books

Anno, M. (1999). *Anno's Magic Seeds.*

Anno, M. (1999). *Anno's Mysterious Multiplying Jar.*

Burns, M. (1996). *How Many Feet? How Many Tails?*

Keenan, S. (2001). *Lizzy's Dizzy Day, Dizzy Day.*

Tang, G. (2002). *The Best of Times.*

Tang, G. (2002). *Math for All Seasons.*

Tang, G. (2003). *Math-terpieces.*

Tang, G. (2004). *Math Fables.*

 ## The Home–School Connection

Mathematical problem solving should take place at home and in the preschool. To involve children's families in mathematical problem-solving activities, teachers might do the following:

- Obtain a copy of *Let's Do Math.* The ideas in this Web resource have been revised in the tear-out sheet on pages 163 and 164 to match the mathematical abilities of children ages 3–5. Put this on your Web page, or duplicate it and send it home to families.

- During conversations with family members at the beginning or end of the day, share with them some of the problems children have been interested in at school and provide suggestions for continuing the exploration at home. For example, if a young child shows great interest in always finding out "how many" there are of things, encourage parents or family members to work with children to count different things around the home.

- Communicate with families about the importance of allowing children to struggle with and even come to incorrect conclusions about problems. Children learn much from mistakes, and parents should encourage children to suggest ways to solve problems. A parent on the subway was overheard asking her young child at which stop they should get off the train. The boy looked up at the digital map that showed each stop and said, "Ummm . . . I think the one that starts with the F, right? No, that can't be it because there's no M train there. Oh! The next stop has the M train. That's the one." The parent responded, "That sounds good. So, when we get off I'll follow you, OK?" Obviously, it's not always efficient to follow children's leads, but allowing them the opportunity to observe, reflect, and come up with conclusions on their own validates their thought processes.

◇ **Documenting and Assessing Children's Learning**

Differing forms of observing can be employed to evaluate and assess young children's development of problem-solving skills, as follows:

- During the day, observe children during work and play time. Record their observations of attributes or events and whether they ask related questions. Note the type of question and whether they waited for a response or tried to answer the question themselves or with others. You should see children developing problem-solving skills in these ways:

  - Observing and making comments; following comments with simple questions or actions

  - Moving from asking questions in wonder ("Why is the sky blue?") to questions with a purpose ("How can these fit?")

  - Asking questions that relate directly to observed phenomena or collected data

  - Noticing mathematical problems and using previous information and/or appropriate strategies to try to answer questions on their own

- Document children's approaches to problems and help children reflect on the processes:

  - When children work to solve problems, take a picture of the end result and ask children how they solved the problem. Record strategies, failed attempts, and thought processes. Keep track of the strategies children use, observing whether they adapt and no longer use strategies that failed before, or reuse strategies that worked.

  - Encourage children to document their own problem solving methods. Older children especially are capable of explaining their thinking by using images to represent the processes they used to solve problems. Teachers may take dictation for children to help clarify the pictures.

─────────────── **FOR THE CHILDREN** ───────────────

Mathematical problem solving is an integral part of children's daily lives. It is the job of the teacher to identify the math problems children experience, to support and guide children through the problem-solving process, and to help children document and reflect on their results.

◇ **Project Work**

Children learn best when their minds and bodies are actively engaged in meaningful experiences. Project, thematic, or unit work offers children the best opportunity to be engaged in this way. Whatever the theme or topic, you can integrate the significant mathematical problem-solving processes and skills of questioning, observing, comparing, and contrasting. Throughout, children will experience the following aspects of problem solving:

- Understanding that there is a problem

- Planning how to solve the problem

- Carrying out the plan

- Reviewing the solution

1. Children Will Develop the Ability to Make Careful Observations and Comment on Phenomena

Children can be astute observers. In quality preschool programs, natural observing skills are expanded and extended. The process of refining children's observation skills includes observing number and other mathematic concepts. Classrooms should be equipped with tools that encourage observation as well as interesting materials for children to observe, such as magnifying glasses, bug boxes, specimen jars, color paddles, and small insects, worms, and plants.

◆ Opportunities to observe occur indoors and outdoors. While on a community walk or out on the playground, notice with children the number of different kinds of plants growing in a given spot. Teachers might give children a hula hoop or a circle of string to place on the ground and have them observe and count the plants inside it. Or, they could count any insect life they find.

◆ Observe insects. Really look at them. How many wings, eyes, and legs do they have? Now ask children to really look at spiders. How many eyes, wings, and legs do they have? Create a Venn diagram with children documenting similarities and differences between spiders and insects.

◆ As children observe insects, introduce the idea of symmetry. Using a specimen, place a file card over one half of the insect. Ask children to predict what the covered side looks like. If they have observed insects carefully and thoughtfully, they'll tell you it's just like the side they can see. Purchase ladybugs from a science supply shop and observe how symmetrical they are.

◆ Find and bring a caterpillar to the group. Place it on a piece of clear plastic and ask children to really look at it. How many eyes does the caterpillar have? How many legs? Are any of the parts symmetrical? Hold the plastic above the children and ask them to observe how the caterpillar moves. How many legs move at a time?

2. Children Begin to Organize Information in Representational Ways

Project work begins with a question or problem to be solved. The question can come from the teacher, who observes, listens to, and questions children to determine their interests, or it can come from a child or group of children.

In a 5-year-old classroom, children were confronted with a real-life problem (*Shoe & Meter*, 1997). The classroom needed another worktable, and the teacher wanted a table identical to the other tables in the classroom. The children suggested that a carpenter would be able to build them a new table, but the carpenter said that he needed the exact measurements before he could make a new table.

MODELING QUESTIONING SKILLS

Every day, teachers model questioning. They frequently ask children questions like these: Why is this nut and bolt heavier than this larger acorn? Who is tallest? Who has the longest piece of yarn? How many times can you jump? How far can you jump? Which of these is heaviest? Which is smallest?

Because teachers want children to develop mathematical problem-solving strategies, they should frequently ask children about the strategies they used to solve problems:

- How did you figure that out?
- Is there another way you could find out?
- How do you know that is the answer?
- What are you thinking about?
- Are you finding an answer? Have you tried thinking another way?
- Are you sure?
- What would happen if . . . ?
- Were you surprised by this?

Rather than solving this problem for the children, the teacher allowed them to struggle with it, knowing that they had limited formal measurement experiences. The children had many different ideas, including using numbers and fingers and hands to measure, and drawing pictures to show how they want the table to be. The teacher guided them with questions and recorded questions the children asked. Some questions involved whether the carpenter was really able to build a table just like the ones in their room. The children thought that drawing the table first would help them communicate their needs to the carpenter. Following this lead, the teacher suggested they use the actual table to help take measurements. They decided to use their bodies to measure the table—fingers, hands, fists, heads, arms, and legs—and kept a record of the number of each body part they used. They realized it was more efficient to use longer body parts and eventually made the transition to other objects, such as ladles and books. They quickly found that certain objects lent themselves more readily to measurement than others.

3. Children Will Analyze Data and Ask New, Related Questions

As the teachers observed the children, they realized that measuring the table accurately would require more experience with measurement processes. They asked some of the children how they would measure a jump from one place to another. A child suggested that the starting point and the end point should be marked. Then, the distance could be measured by taking steps from one point to the other. After one child jumped and the distance was marked, another child walked toe to toe and found that the jump was four "feet" long. In order to challenge the children's thinking, the teacher measured using her steps and found that it was three "feet" long. She continued to measure after the children jumped and did their own measurements, and hers were consistently "shorter" than the other children's measurements. They finally figured out that it was because her feet were bigger and "take up more space." Understanding the concept of using a consistent unit of measure is essential to accurate measurement.

When questioning children about their problem-solving strategies, the teacher is interested in the strategy more than in the answer.

4. Children Will Use Data to Reach Conclusions

Once the children understood that feet were reliable tools for measuring, one child volunteered his shoe to measure the table. They carefully placed the shoe repeatedly along the length of the table and discovered it was six and a half shoes long. Repeating the process on the width, they found that the measurement for the "shortness" was three shoes. This realization—that the shoe could be used as a reliable measure—was very exciting for children. But they also quickly realized that they could not give the carpenter the boy's shoe. This led them to finally pull out a measuring stick to measure the shoe and to calculate the length and width based on that measurement. Then they documented the numbers alongside the outlines of the shoes and had a clear representation of the measurement of the top of the table.

Some children joined and left the discussion, while a core group followed it through. But the interest in measurement permeated the classroom, with other opportunities to measure being realized as children worked on other projects. Encouraging children to use data to reach conclusions should be a regular part of daily activities.

◆ As children work on projects in different learning areas, look for opportunities to model data analysis and to help children draw conclusions.

- In the art area, use recipes to make play dough. Model for children the observation of how much flour is just the right amount—too little means sticky dough, and too much means dough that is difficult to manipulate. Encourage children to record the optimal amounts of flour and water.

- Take an inventory of the classroom materials that children most often and least often play with. Discuss strategies for removing some materials or reorganizing them so children have better access to them.

◆ Use spontaneous experiences. During daily living, there will be many opportunities for children to observe data and draw conclusions.

- When two children are painting at easels, you might ask them to count and compare the number of colors used in each of their paintings.

- One classroom bought ladybugs for their garden. After the insects were released, the children counted the ladybugs each saw and recorded their counts. Then they compared how many ladybugs they each saw in their garden the next day.

- "He has more," complains Tonja. When this happens, count and compare how many blocks, puzzle pieces, dolls, or books children have at a given time. Use this information to determine a fair sharing rule for the class.

- "I can make a longer snake than you," says Antonio, working at the clay table rolling and rolling a snake. The other children can join in comparing who made the longest snake and the shortest.

5. Children Will Gain Skills in Reflecting

Children can represent their problem-solving strategies through drawings, paintings, or construction. Drawing, painting, or representing their math work in some other concrete way forces children to think, rethink, evaluate, and reflect on their work. It is important that teachers and other children take part in the reflection process, validating children's efforts and thinking.

Larry Buschman uses a "mathematician's chair" with his class, where children are given the opportunity to share and discuss their strategies and solutions with others. This is a safe space for children to think out loud and for the community to learn together about math concepts, strategies, and differences of thought and opinion. The teacher's role during the mathematician's chair is to listen to the student and learn from the explanations, encourage children to engage in the conversation, focus on the strategies rather than just the final solution, and ask guiding questions to help children express themselves clearly. The teacher also models active listening, which requires attention to the speaker, restating what the speaker has said in your own words, responding to the speaker with relevant comments or questions, and thinking ahead to what the speaker might say next.

Before children share in front of the class, they are given the opportunity to share their strategies with another child. This encourages cooperative learning and also allows children to try out their strategies, revise and edit, and clarify their thinking before sharing with the rest of the class. The key to respectful dialogue is that children agree or disagree with the speaker, rather than trying to determine who has arrived at the correct solution. This contributes to the sense of safety and allows all children the freedom to

Children use different strategies to solve problems.

share without fear of being labeled as "wrong." Finally, when each child finishes his or her time in the mathematician's chair, the rest of the class shows their appreciation for the child's efforts by applause.

Different children will want to represent their strategies and to reflect on them in different ways. Here are some other suggestions for helping children to develop reflecting skills:

◆ Start keeping math journals. Teachers might start by making a big math journal for the group, modeling the ways we can record our thoughts, document and organize data, write questions, and reflect on strategies and solutions. In the journal, keep a record of important questions children ask during work time, as well as methods for finding solutions; record tallies for votes on important classroom topics; and write down concepts children appear to be curious about.

Children in prekindergarten can begin to keep their own math journals, which they may use in different ways:

- To record math ideas they know

- To represent questions or answers to questions

- To write numbers or number problems that are meaningful to them

- To represent figures or structures they have created or to create new designs using shapes

◆ Make math murals.

- Take a neighborhood walk, observing the environment, special buildings or parks, and interesting homes. Work with children to recreate the school neighborhood on a mural, paying attention to places which are closer to or farther away from the school building and highlighting any of the children's homes that may be in the same neighborhood.

- Make murals of children's growth and development. Divide a sheet of mural paper into two sections. Label the sections "When I Was a Baby" and "Now I'm Big." Children record their weight as a baby and their current weight and draw pictures of themselves.

◇ Extending and Expanding to the Primary Grades

Children who have had many positive experiences with problem solving and have been exposed to teachers modeling the process during the early years not only will adjust to that approach in the primary grades, but will ask for problems to solve. Problem solving is a powerful approach to math teaching that engages students in the processes used by mathematicians, and it should be collaborative and supportive for all children. Some excellent books for applying a problem-solving approach were listed earlier in this chapter. Teachers should expose children to the Anno books; the author provides suggestions in the back for how the books might be used to strengthen math reasoning and concepts. Other children's books provide a good basis from which to begin to solve a problem. For instance:

- Read *Math for All Seasons* by Gregory Tang. With seasonal themes, these rhyming math puzzles and number problems encourage children to think through problems rather than relying on memorization. The poetry and drawings are fun and creative and support the process over the solution. Solutions and explanations are provided in the back of the book. This book can be used over and over again and in different ways.

- Read *Math-terpieces* by Gregory Tang. Here Tang uses the artwork of 12 famous painters to develop children's problem-solving skills through grouping. Clearly written solutions are given at the end of the book.

- Children in the primary grades would be attracted to Journey North, a global study of wildlife migration and seasonal change. This free Internet-based program (www.learner.org/jnorth/) allows children to share their observations with other children across North America. As they study a migrating species—whales or monarch butterflies—or when emperor tulips bloom, children will apply every mathematical skill and concept and fulfill every standard of the National Council of Teachers of Mathematics.

Everyday experiences abound with opportunities for children to solve problems. Mr. Buschman's class was presented with the following problem: He wanted to give two cards to each child in the class, and there were five cards in each packet. So how many packets did he need to buy? Mr. Buschman encouraged the children to solve the problem in a way that made sense to them personally. Because of this, the children approached the problem in many different ways, some using numbers or tallies, others drawing pictures of children and cards.

The children all recorded their solutions, using words and pictures. During the mathematician's chair, the children shared their solutions, and Mr. Buschman asked careful questions, such as:

- How did you figure it out?

- Why does your way of solving the problem get the answer?

- How do you know it works?

- How many circles and how many squares do you predict Marissa will draw?

- What do you mean by "twice that many?"

- Could you show the class how you solved the problem using the cubes and tiles?

Older children can record their solutions on overhead pages first, so that the class can observe and think more critically about the strategies. This allows children to see that solutions can be recorded in alternative ways.

To assess children's learning, the teacher may group children into four categories, as follows:

1. Can figure out problems by counting or using an involved strategy
2. Is beginning to use efficient strategies, but may not explain them clearly
3. Knows how to use efficient strategies, but may not always explain them clearly
4. Knows how to use efficient strategies, regularly explains them clearly

The experiences may be extended by giving the children larger numbers so that they can make estimates. Or, teachers may challenge the children by providing the answer and asking for the question, such as Barlow and Cates (2006) in their article "The Answer Is 20 Cookies. What Is the Question?" The answer did not have to be 20 cookies—rather, it could be 18 pigs or 50 cents. Here, students were asked to create their own word problems. The authors found that it was necessary to give specific instructions and that the inclusion of units such as cookies helped children to formulate word problems. Once understood, the task provides the opportunity for children to come up with a variety of word problems and demonstrate their creativity.

Let's Solve Problems Together!

You use math to solve problems every day. Here are some ways to help involve your children in these daily problem-solving experiences:

At the grocery store:

- Before you go, make a grocery list. Talk about how much the items cost, and include the items on your grocery list.

- As you shop at the store, remind your children to shop for the items they've selected.

- Ask children to select as many apples as are needed for the desired weight, or put one apple in the bag for each person in the family.

- When you're back from the store, children can:

  - Help you put groceries away, sort the foods by type, or put them on the correct shelf with other like foods

  - Count and sort the number of fruits, vegetables, cans, or jars you've purchased

Encourage children to think about numbers:

- Play number games with children, from This Little Piggy to bingo, card games, and board games.

- Let children see you solve problems by counting, adding, or subtracting: "I need two more cups." "Help me button the last one." "How many more do I need?" "I have too many. What should I do?"

- Show children when writing numbers is helpful, for example when writing down a phone number, addressing an envelope, or writing a check to pay a bill. Encourage children to write numbers for their own purposes.

Use toys to think about problem solving:

Balls

- Which ball is the largest? The smallest? Which one do you think will bounce the highest/roll the furthest?

- Which balls float? Let's try them in this bucket of water.

- How do balls behave when rolled on the grass, ground, and sidewalk?

Blocks

- Let's see who can build the tallest tower.

- How many circle blocks are there?

- How many blocks do you think will fit inside this square?

- Can we make a house big enough for your car/doll/teddy bear?

Boxes

- Which box is the largest/smallest?

- Can we put these boxes in order from smallest to biggest?

- How many boxes can you stack before they fall?

- How many smaller boxes fit inside the larger box?

Share household chores. For instance:

- Sort laundry. Children can sort their own clothes and take them to their rooms, as well as clothes belonging to other members of the family. This helps them think about attributes and patterns.

- Set the table. By setting the table, children think about patterns, such as fork, plate, knife, cup.

- Empty the dishwasher. As children sort silverware into the appropriate slots of the drawer, they think about how the forks, spoons, and knives are the same or different and learn to pay attention to important attributes.

References

Andrews, A. G., & Trafton, P. R. (2002). *Little kids, powerful problem solvers: Math stories from a kindergarten classroom.* Portsmouth, NH: Heinemann.

Balfanz, R., Ginsburg, H. P., & Greenes, C. (2003). The Big Math for Little Kids early childhood mathematics program. *Teaching Children Mathematics, 9*(5), 264–268.

Barbour, N., & Seefeldt, C. (1993). *Developmental continuity across preschool and primary grades.* Olney, MD: Association for Childhood Education International.

Barlow, A. T., & Cates, J. M. (2006). The answer is 20 cookies. What is the question? *Teaching Children Mathematics, 13*(5), 252–255.

Barnett, W. S., Epstein, D. J., Friedman, A. H., Stevenson-Boyd, J., & Hustedt, J. T. (2009). *The state of preschool 2008: State preschool yearbook.* New Brunswick, NJ: National Institute for Early Education Research.

Baroody, A. J., & Wilkins, J. L. M. (1999). The development of informal counting, number, and arithmetic skills and concepts in the primary grades. In J. V. Copley (Ed.), *Mathematics in the early years* (pp. 48–65). Reston, VA: National Council of Teachers of Mathematics; Washington, DC: National Association for the Education of Young Children.

Basile, C. (1999). The outdoors as a context for mathematics in the early years. In J. V. Copley (Ed.), *Mathematics in the early years* (pp. 150–161). Reston, VA: National Council of Teachers of Mathematics; Washington, DC: National Association for the Education of Young Children.

Berk, L. E., & Winsler, A. (1995). *Scaffolding children's learning: Vygotsky and early childhood education.* Washington, DC: National Association for the Education of Young Children.

Blaska, J. K., & Lynch, E. C. (1998). Is everyone included? Using children's literature to facilitate the understanding of disabilities. *Young Children, 53*(2), 36–40.

Bodrova, E., & Leong, D. (2007). Play and early literacy: A Vygotskian approach. In K. A. Roskos & J. F. Christie (Eds.), *Play and literacy in early childhood* (2nd ed). Mahwah, NJ: Erlbaum.

Bredekamp, S. (1993, November). Reflections on Reggio Emilia. Young Children, *49*(1), 13–17.

Bredekamp, S., & Rosegrant, T. (1995). *Reaching potentials: Transforming early childhood curriculum and assessment* (Vol. 2). Washington, DC: National Association for the Education of Young Children.

Bronfenbrenner, U. (1979). *The ecology of human development: Experiments by nature and design.* Cambridge, MA: Harvard University Press.

Bronson, M. B. (1995). *The right stuff for children birth to 8: Selecting play materials to support development.* Washington, DC: National Association for the Education of Young Children.

Bruner, J. (1966). *Toward a theory of instruction.* Cambridge, MA: Belknap Press.

Buschman, L. (2003). *Share and compare: A teacher's story about helping children become problem solvers in mathematics.* Reston, VA: National Council of Teachers of Mathematics.

Burns, M. (1993). *Math and literature (K–3).* Sausalito, CA: Marilyn Burns Education Associates.

Charlesworth, R. (2012). *Experiences in math for young children* (6th ed.). Boston: Wadsworth

Charlesworth, R., Hart, C. H., Burts, D. C., & DeWolf, M. (1993). The LSU studies: Building a research base for developmentally appropriate practice. In S. Reifel (Ed.), *Perspectives on developmentally appropriate practice: Vol. 5. Advances in early education and day care* (pp. 3–28). Greenwich, CT: JAI Press.

Charlesworth, R., & Radeloff, D. J. (1978). *Experiences in math for young children.* Albany, NY: Delmar.

Chrisman, K. (2005). The nuts and bolts of discovery centers. *Science and Children, 43*(3), 21–23.

Clements, D. H. (1999b). Geometric and spatial thinking in young children. In J. V. Copley (Ed.), *Mathematics in the early years* (pp. 66–79). Reston, VA: National Council of Teachers of Mathematics; Washington, DC: National Association for the Education of Young Children.

Clements, D. H., DiBiase, A-M., & Sarama, J. (eds.). (2004). Engaging young children in mathematics: Standards for early childhood mathematics education. Mahwah, NJ: Erlbaum.

Clements, D. H., & Sarama, J. (2006, October). Your child's mathematical mind. *Parent & Child,* 30–39.

Clements, D. H., & Sarama, J. (2007a). *Building Blocks.* Early childhood mathematics learning. In F. K. Lester (ed.), Second Handbook of Research on Mathematics Teaching and Learning (pp. 461–555). New York: Information Age.

Clements, D. H., & Sarama, J. (2007b). Effects of a preschool mathematics curriculum: Summative research on the *Building Blocks* project. *Journal for Research in Mathematics Education, 38*(2), 136–163.

Clements, D. H., & Sarama, J. (2007c). Effects of a preschool mathematics curriculum: Summative research on the *Building Blocks* project. *Journal for Research in Mathematics Education, 38,* 136–163.

Clements, D. H., & Sarama, J. (2009). *Learning and teaching early math: The learning trajectories approach.* New York: Routledge.

Copley, J. V. (2000). *The young child and mathematics.* Reston, VA: National Council of Teachers of Mathematics; Washington, DC: National Association for the Education of Young Children.

Copley, J., & Padrón, Y. (1999). Preparing teachers of young learners: Professional development of early childhood teachers in mathematics and science. In *Dialogue on early childhood science, mathematics, and technology education.* Washington, DC: Project 2061, American Association for the Advancement of Science.

Curcio, F. R. (2010). *Developing graph comprehension.* Reston, VA: National Council of Teachers of Mathematics.

Cutler, K. M., Gilkerson, D., Parrott, S., & Browne, M. T. (2003). Developing math games based on children's literature. *Young Children, 58*(1), 22–27.

Damon, W., & Phelps, E. (1989). Critical distinctions among three approaches to peer education. *International Journal of Educational Research, 13,* 9–19.

Davila Coates, G., & Thompson, V. (1999). Involving parents of four- and five-year-olds in their children's mathematics education: The FAMILY MATH experience. In J. V. Copley (Ed.), *Mathematics in the early years* (pp. 198–214). Reston, VA: National Council of Teachers of Mathematics.

de Vise, D. (2006, December 5). Local schools to study whether Math − Topics = Better instruction. *The Washington Post,* p. A1.

Dewey, J. (1938). *Experience and education.* New York: Collier Books.

Dewey, J. (1944). *Democracy and education.* New York: Free Press.

Diamond, A., Barnett, S. W., Thomas, J., & Munro, S. (2007). Preschool program improves cognitive control. *Science, 318,* 1387–1388.

Dighe, J., Calomiris, Z., & Van Zutphen, C. (1998). Nurturing the language of art in children. *Young Children, 53*(1), 4–9.

Duncan, G. J., Dowsett, C. J., Claessens, A., Magnusson, K., Huston, A. C., Klebanov, P., et al. (2007). School readiness and later achievement. *Developmental Psychology, 43,* 1428–1446.

Dyson, A. H. (1987). The value of time off-task: Young children's spontaneous talk and deliberate text. *Harvard Educational Review, 57*(4), 396–420.

Findell, C. R., Small, M., Cavanagh, M., Dacey, L., Greenes, C. E., & Shellfield, L. J. (2001). *Navigating through geometry in prekindergarten–grade 2 (with CD-ROM).* Reston, VA: National Council of Teachers of Mathematics.

Flynn, L. L., & Kieff, J. (2002). Including everyone in outdoor play. *Young Children, 57*(3), 20–26.

Fromboluti, C. S., Rinck, N., Magarity, D., & Gibson, B. (1999). *Early childhood: Where learning begins—Mathematics: Mathematical activities for parents and their 2- to 5-year-old children.* Washington, DC: U.S. Department of Education, National Institute on Early Childhood Development and Education.

Geist, E. (2003). Infants and toddlers exploring mathematics. *Young Children, 58*(1), 10–12.

Gerdes, P. (1999). *Geometry from Africa: Mathematical and educational explorations.* Washington, DC: Mathematical Association of America.

Ginsburg, H. P. (2006). Mathematical play and playful mathematics: A guide for early education. In D. Singer, R. M. Golinkoff & K. Hirsh-Pasek (Eds.), *Play = Learning: How play motivates and enhances children's cognitive and social-emotional growth* (pp. 145–165). New York: Oxford University Press.

Ginsburg, H. P. (2009). The challenge of formative assessment in mathematics education: Children's minds, teachers' minds. *Human Development, 52*(2), 109–128.

Ginsburg, H. P., & Amit, M. (2008). What is teaching mathematics to young children? A theoretical perspective and case study. *Journal of Applied Developmental Psychology, 29,* 274–285.

Ginsburg, H. P., Greenes, C., & Balfanz, R. (2003). *Big math for little kids.* Parsippany, NJ: Dale Seymour.

Ginsburg, H. P., Lee, J. S., & Boyd, J. S. (2008). Mathematics education for young children: What it is and how to promote it. *Society for Research in Child Development Social Policy Report, 22,* 1–23.

Ginsburg, H. P., Pappas, S., & Seo, K.-H. (2001). Everyday mathematical knowledge: Asking young children what is developmentally appropriate. In S. L. Golbeck (Ed.), *Psychological perspectives on early childhood education: Reframing dilemmas in research and practice* (pp. 180–216). Mahwah, NJ: Erlbaum.

Greenes, C. (1999a). The Boston University–Chelsea Project. In J. V. Copley (Ed.), *Mathematics in the early years* (pp. 151–155). Reston, VA: National Council of Teachers of Mathematics; Washington, DC: National Association for the Education of Young Children.

Greenes, C. (1999b). Ready to learn: Developing young children's mathematical powers. In J. V. Copley (Ed.), *Mathematics in the early years* (pp. 39–47). Reston, VA: National Council of Teachers of Mathematics; Washington, DC: National Association for the Education of Young Children.

Greenes, C., Cavanagh, M., Dacey, L., Findell, C., & Small, M. (2001). *Navigating through algebra in prekindergarten–grade 2 (with CD-ROM).* Reston, VA: National Council of Teachers of Mathematics.

Greenman, J. (2007). *Caring spaces, learning places.* St. Paul, MN: Redleaf Press.

Griffin, S. (2007). *Number worlds: A mathematics intervention program for grades preK–6.* Columbus, OH: SRA/McGraw-Hill.

Harms, T., Clifford, R. M, & Cryer, D. (2005). *The Early Childhood Environment Rating Scale–Revised.* New York: Teachers College Press.

Hohmann, M., & Weikart, D. P. (2002). *Educating young children: Active learning practices for preschool and child care* (2nd ed.). Ypsilanti, MI: High/Scope Press.

Huber, L. L., & Lenhoff, R. S. (2006, November). Early childhood corner: Mathematical concepts come alive in pre-K and kindergarten classrooms. *Teaching Children Mathematics, 13(4),* 226–231.

Hurst, C. O., & Otis, R. (1996). *Picturing math.* Worthington, OH: SRA/McGraw-Hill.

Jenkins, E. (1989). *You'll sing a song and I'll sing a song* [CD]. Smithsonian Folkways Recordings.

Jenkins, E. (1994). *This is rhythm* [CD]. Smithsonian Folkways Recordings.

Jenkins, E. (1996). *Jambo and other call-and-response songs and chants* [CD]. Smithsonian Folkways Recordings.

Johnson-Foote, B. (2001). *Cup cooking.* Beltsville, MD: Gryphon House.

Jones, J., & Courtney, R. (2002). Documenting early science learning. *Young Children, 50*(5), 34–40.

Katz, L. (1993). What can we learn from Reggio Emilia? In C. Edwards, L. Gandini, & G. Forman (Eds.), *The hundred languages of children* (pp. 19–41). Norwood, NJ: Ablex.

Kim, S. L. (1999). Teaching mathematics through musical activities. In J. V. Copley (Ed.), *Mathematics in the early years* (pp. 146–150). Reston, VA: National Council of Teachers of Mathematics; Washington, DC: National Association for the Education of Young Children.

Klibanoff, R., Levine, S. C., Huttenlocher, J., Vasilyeva, M., & Hedges, L. (2006). Preschool children's mathematical knowledge: The effect of teacher "math talk." *Developmental Psychology, 42,* 59–69.

Kohl, M. A., & Gainer, C. (1997). *Math arts: Exploring math through art for 3 to 6 year olds.* Beltsville, MD: Gryphon House.

Lee, M., & Miller, M. (1999). *Great graphing.* New York: Scholastic.

Lester, F. K., & Charles, R. I. (2003). *Teaching mathematics through problem solving: Pre-kindergarten–grade 6.* Reston, VA: National Council of Teachers of Mathematics.

Lobman, C., Ryan, S., & McLaughlin, J. (2005). Reconstructing teacher education to prepare qualified preschool teachers: Lessons from New Jersey. *Early Childhood Research & Practice, 7*(2).

Mallory, B. L. (1998). Educating young children with developmental differences: Principles of inclusive practice. In C. Seefeldt & A. Galper (Eds.), *Continuing issues in early childhood education* (2nd ed., p. 228). Upper Saddle River, NJ: Merrill/Prentice Hall.

Marcon, R. (1992). Differential effects of three preschool models on inner-city 4-year-olds. *Early Childhood Research Quarterly, 7*(4), 517–530.

Marcon, R. (2002). Moving up the grades: Relationship between preschool model and later school success. *Early Childhood Research and Practice, 4*(1).

Maryland State Department of Education (MSDE). (1992). *Laying the foundation for the future.* Baltimore: Author.

Marzolf, D. P., & DeLoache, J. S. (1994). Transfer in young children's understanding of spatial representations. *Child Development, 65*(1), 1–15.

McAfee, O., Leong, D., & Bodrova, E. (2004). *Basics of assessment: Primer for early childhood educators.* Washington, DC: National Association for the Education of Young Children.

National Association for the Education of Young Children (NAEYC) & National Council of Teachers of Mathematics (NCTM). (2002). *Early childhood mathematics: Promoting good beginnings.* Joint position statement. Washington, DC, and Reston, VA: Authors. Available at www.naeyc.org/files/naeyc/file/positions/psmath.pdf

National Council of Teachers of Mathematics (NCTM). (1989). *Curriculum and evaluation standards for school mathematics.* Reston, VA: Author.

National Council of Teachers of Mathematics (NCTM). (2000). *Principles and standards for school mathematics.* Reston, VA: Author.

National Council of Teachers of Mathematics (NCTM). (2002). *The mathematics education of `underrepresented groups.* Reston, VA: Author. Available at www.nctm.org/about/content.aspx?id=6366

National Council of Teachers of Mathematics (NCTM). (2006). *Curriculum focal points for prekindergarten through grade 8 mathematics: A quest for coherence.* Reston, VA: Author.

National Council of Teachers of Mathematics (NCTM). (2007). *Algebra in the early grades.* Mahwah, NJ: Erlbaum.

National Council of Teachers of Mathematics (NCTM), Craine, T., & Rubenstein, R. (2009). *Understanding Geometry for a Changing World.* Reston, VA: NCTM.

National Research Council (NRC). (2001). *Adding it up: Helping children learn mathematics.* J. Kilpatrick, J. Swafford, & B. Findell (Eds.). Mathematics Learning Study Committee, Center for Education, Division for Behavioral and Social Sciences and Education. Washington, DC: National Academies Press.

National Research Council. (2010). *Mathematics Learning in Early Childhood: Paths Toward Excellence and Equity.* C. T. Cross, T. A. Woods, & H. Schweingruber (Eds.). Washington, DC: National Academies Press.

O'Connell, S. (2007). *Introduction to problem solving, Grades PreK–2* (2nd ed.). Portsmouth, NH: Heinemann.

Orlando, L. (1993). *The multicultural game book.* New York: Scholastic.

Paley, V. G. (2004). *A child's play: The importance of fantasy play.* Chicago: University of Chicago Press.

Patilla, P. (1999). *Math links series: Measuring.* Portsmouth, NH: Heinemann.

Payne, J. N. (Ed.). (1990). *Mathematics for the young child.* Reston, VA: National Council of Teachers of Mathematics.

Piaget, J. (1970). *The child's concept of number.* New York: Viking Press.

Piaget, J., & Inhelder, B. (1969). *The psychology of the child.* New York: Basic Books.

Polonsky, L. (Ed.). (2000). *Math for the very young: A handbook of activities for parents and teachers.* New York: Wiley.

Riley-Ayers, S., Stevenson-Garcia, J., Frede, E., & Brenneman, K. (2009). *The Early Learning Scale.* New Brunswick, NJ: National Institute for Early Education Research.

Sarama, J., & Clements, D. H. (2006). Mathematics in kindergarten. *Young Children, 61*(5), 38–41.

Sarama, J., & Clements, D. H. (2009). *Early childhood mathematics education research: Learning trajectories for young children.* New York: Routledge.

Sarama, J., Clements, D. H., Starkey, P., Klein, A., & Wakeley, A. (2008). Scaling up the implementation of a pre-kindergarten mathematics curriculum: Teaching for understanding with trajectories and technologies. *Journal of Research on Educational Effectiveness, 1*(2), 89–119.

Schiller, P., & Peterson, L. (1997). *Count on math: Activities for small hands and lively minds.* Beltsville, MD: Gryphon House.

Seefeldt, C. (1993). Learning for freedom. *Young Children, 48*(3), 4–9.

Seefeldt, C. (1995). Art: A serious work. *Young Children, 50*(3), 39–54.

Seefeldt, C. (1997). *Social studies for the preschool–primary child.* Upper Saddle River, NJ: Merrill/Prentice Hall.

Seefeldt, C. (2005). *How to work with standards in the early childhood classroom.* New York: Teachers College Press.

Seefeldt, C., & Barbour, N. (1998). *Early childhood education: An introduction.* Upper Saddle River, NJ: Merrill/Prentice Hall.

Seefeldt, C., & Galper, A. (2007). *Active experiences for active children:* Science (2nd ed.). Upper Saddle River, NJ: Merrill/Prentice Hall.

Seo, K. (2003). What children's play tells us about teaching mathematics. *Young Children, 58*(1), 28–34.

Seo, K-H., & Ginsburg, H. P. (2004).What is developmentally appropriate in early mathematics education? Lessons from new research. In D. Clements, J. Sarama, & A. diBiase (Eds.), *Engaging young children in mathematics: Standards for early childhood mathematics education* (pp. 91–104). Mahwah, NJ: Erlbaum.

Starkey, P., Klein, A., & Wakeley, A. (2004). Enhancing young children's mathematical knowledge through a pre-kindergarten mathematics intervention. *Early Childhood Research Quarterly, 19*(1), 99–120.

Stenmark, J. K., & Coates, G. D. (1997). *Family Math for Young Children: Comparing.* New York: Equals.

Stenmark, J. K., Thompson, V., & Cossey, R. (1986). *Family math.* New York: Equals.

Taylor-Cox, J. (2003). Algebra in the early years? Yes! *Young Children, 58*(1), 14–21.

Thiessen, D., Matthias, M., & Smith, J. (1998). *Wonderful world of mathematics: A critically annotated list of children's books in mathematics* (2nd ed.). Reston, VA: National Council of Teachers of Mathematics.

Thomas, B. (1982). *An abstract of kindergarten teachers' elicitation and utilization of children's prior knowledge in the teaching of shape concepts:* Unpublished manuscript, School of Education, Health, Nursing, and Arts Professions, New York University.

U.S. Department of Education. (n.d.). *Let's do math* [Pamphlet]. Washington, DC: Author.

Vygotsky, L. (1978). *Thought and language.* Cambridge, MA: MIT Press.

Vygotsky, L. (1986). *Thought and language* (Rev. ed.). Cambridge, MA: MIT Press.

Whitin, P., & Whitin, D. J. (2003). Developing mathematical understanding along the yellow brick road. *Young Children, 58*(1), 36–39.

Wilson, R. A. (1995). Nature and young children: A natural connection. *Young Children, 50*(6), 4–7.

Wright, J. L., & Shade, D. (Eds.). (1994). *Young children: Active learners in a technological age.* Washington, DC: National Association for the Education of Young Children.

Youniss, J., & Damon, W. (1992). Social construction of Piaget's theory. In H. Beilin & P. B. Pufall (Eds.), *Piaget's theory: Perspectives and possibilities.* Hillsdale, NJ: Erlbaum.

Children's Books

Aardema, V. (1975). *Why mosquitoes buzz in people's ears.* New York: Dial Books for Young Readers.

Adler, D. A. (1999). *How tall, how short, how faraway.* New York: Holiday House.

Anno, M. (1977). *Anno's math games.* New York: Putnam.

Anno, M. (1986). *Anno's counting book.* New York: HarperTrophy.

Anno, M. (1999). *Anno's magic seeds.* New York: Paper Star.

Anno, M. (1999). *Anno's mysterious multiplying jar.* Putnam Juvenile.

Baker, K. (2004). *Quack and count.* New York: Voyager Books.

Bang, M. (2003). *Ten, nine, eight/Diez, nueve, ocho.* New York: HarperTrophy.

Barton, B. (1991). *The three bears.* New York: HarperFestival.

Base, G. (2006). *Uno's garden.* New York: Abrams Books for Young Readers.

Blackstone, S. (2009). *Bear in a square/Oso en un cuadrado.* Cambridge, MA: Barefoot Books.

Brown, M. W. (1947). *Goodnight moon/Buenas noches luna.* New York: Harper & Row.

Burns, M. (1994). *The greedy triangle.* New York: Scholastic.

Burns, M. (1996). *How many feet? How many tails?* New York: Scholastic.

Carle, E. (1986). *The secret birthday message.* New York: HarperTrophy.

Carle, E. (1994). *The very hungry caterpillar.* London: Hamish Hamilton.

Carle, E. (1996). *The grouchy ladybug.* New York: HarperCollins/HarperFestival.

Clements, A. (2006). *A million dots.* New York: Simon & Shuster Children's.

Crews, D. (1995). *Ten black dots/Diez puntos negros.* New York: Mulberry Books.

Dee, R. (1988). *Two ways to count to ten: A Liberian folktale.* New York: Holt.

De Regniers, B. S. (1985). *So many cats!* Wilmington, MA: Houghton Mifflin.

deRubertis, B. (1999). *A collection for Kate.* New York: Kane Press.

Diehl, D. (2007). *A circle here, a square there.* New York: Lark Books.

Dodds, D. A. (1994). *The shape of things.* Cambridge, MA: Candlewick.

Falwell, C. (1993). *Feast for 10/Fiesta para 10.* New York: Clarion Books.

Feelings, M. (1971). *Moja means one: Swahili counting book.* New York: Dial Books.

Fowler, R. (1993). *Ladybug on the move.* New York: Harcourt.

Fox, M. (1990). *Shoes from Grandpa.* London: Orchard Books.

Gerth, M. (2001). *Ten little ladybugs.* New York: Piggy Toes Press.

Greene, R. G. (2001). *When a line bends . . . A shape begins.* Wilmington, MA: Houghton Mifflin.

Grifalconi, V. (1986). *The village of round and square houses.* Boston: Little, Brown.

Grossman, V. (1999). *Ten little rabbits.* New York: Chronicle Books.

Grover, M. (1996). *Circles and squares everywhere.* New York: Harcourt.

Harris, T. (2000). *Pattern fish.* Minneapolis, MN: Millbrook Press.

Hirst, R., & Hirst, S. (1990). *My place in space.* London: Orchard Books.

Hoban, T. (1985). *Is it larger? Is it smaller?* New York: Greenwillow Books.

Hoban, T. (1986). *Shapes, shapes, shapes.* New York: Greenwillow Books.

Hoban, T. (1987). *Dots, spots, speckles, and stripes.* New York: Greenwillow Books.

Hoban, T. (1996). *Circles, triangles, and squares.* New York: Greenwillow Books.

Hoban, T. (2000). *Cubes, cones, cylinders, and spheres.* New York: Greenwillow Books.

Holm, S. L. (2003). *Zoe's hats: A book of colors and patterns.* Honesdale, PA: Boyds Mills Press.

Hopkins, L. B. (Ed.). (1997). *Marvelous math: A book of poems.* New York: Simon & Schuster Children's.

Hutchins, P. (1970). *Clocks and more clocks.* New York: Macmillan.

Hutchins, P. (1986). *The doorbell rang.* New York: Mulberry Books.

Hutchins, P. (1994). *Llaman a la puerta* (A. Marcuse, Trans.). New York: Mulberry Books.

Jenkins, S. (1997). *Biggest, strongest, fastest.* New York: Houghton Mifflin.

Jenkins, S. (2004). *Actual size.* New York: Houghton Mifflin.

Keats, E. J. (1990). *Over in the meadow.* New York: Puffin.

Keenan, S. (2001). *Lizzy's dizzy day, dizzy day.* New York: Cartwheel Books.

Keenan, S., & Girouard, P. (1997). *More or less a mess.* New York: Cartwheel Books.

Krauss, R. (1996). *La semilla de zanahoria.* New York: Scholastic en Español.

Krauss, R. (2004). *The carrot seed.* New York: HarperCollins.

Lionni, L. (1960). *Inch by inch.* New York: Harper Children.

Leedy, L. (2000). *Measuring Penny.* New York: Holt.

Martin, B., Jr. (2008). *Brown bear, brown bear, what do you see?* New York: Henry Holt.

Martin, B., Jr., & Archambault, J. (1989). *Chicka chicka boom boom.* New York: Simon & Schuster Children's.

McKissack, P. C. (1997). *Mirandy and Brother Wind.* New York: Knopf.

McMillan, B. (1986). *Becca backward, Becca forward: A book of concept pairs.* New York: HarperCollins.

Meeks, S. (2002). *Drip drop.* New York: HarperTrophy.

Merriam, E. (1996). *12 ways to get to 11.* New York: Aladdin Paperbacks.

Murphy, S. (1997). *Betcha!* New York: HarperCollins.

Myller, R. (1991). *How big is a foot?* Glenview, IL: Scott Foresman (Pearson K–12).

Numeroff, L. H. (1985). *If you give a mouse a cookie.* New York: HarperCollins.

Pinczes, E. (2001). *Inchworm and a half.* Boston: Houghton Mifflin.

Rathmann, P. (2000). *Goodnight, Gorilla/Buenas noches, Gorila*. New York: Putnam Juvenile.

Reid, M. (1990). *The button box*. New York: Dutton.

Ring, S. (2002). *I see patterns*. Mankato, MN: Red Bricklearning,

Rissman, R. (2009). *Shapes in art (Spot the shape)*. Chicago: Heinemann.

Rissman, R. (2009). *Shapes in buildings (Spot the shape)*. Chicago: Heinemann.

Santomero, A. C. (1998). *The shape detectives*. New York: Simon & Schuster Children's.

Sayre, A. P., & Sayre, J. (2004). *One is a snail, ten is a crab: A counting by feet book*. Cambridge, MA: Candlewick.

Schwartz, D. A. (1985). *How much is a million?* New York: Mulberry Books.

Scieszka, J., & Smith, L. (1995). *Math curse*. New York: Viking Juvenile.

Serfozo, M. (1996). *There's a square: A book about shapes*. New York: Scholastic.

Seuss, Dr. (1988). *The shape of me and other stuff*. New York: Random House.

Shaw, C. G. (1988). *It looked like spilt milk*. New York: HarperTrophy.

Silverstein, S. (1976). *The missing piece*. New York: HarperCollins Children's Books.

Staake, B. (2006). *The red lemon*. New York: Random House.

Swinburne, S. R. (2002). *Lots and lots of zebra stripes: Patterns in nature*. Honesdale, PA: Boyds Mills Press.

Tang, G. (2002). *The best of times*. New York: Scholastic.

Tang, G. (2002). *Math for all seasons*. New York: Scholastic.

Tang, G. (2003). *Math-terpieces*. New York: Scholastic.

Tang, G. (2004). *Math fables*. New York: Scholastic.

Tompert, A. (1990). *Grandfather Tang's story*. New York: Crown.

Tompert, A. (2000). Just a little bit. New York: Scholastic.

Viorst, J. (1988). *Alexander, who used to be rich last Sunday*. New York: Aladdin Books.

Wing, R. W. (1963). *What is big?* New York: Holt, Rinehart & Winston.

Wood, J. (1992). *Moo, moo, brown cow*. New York: Gulliver Books.

Resources

Organizations and Web Sites

All Web sites listed in this book were verified at the time of publication. We have every reason to believe that they will remain valid, but please verify them before sharing with others.

For Teachers

The following Web sites provide valuable resources for teachers of children of all ages. Some sites are specific to math teaching and learning; others contain resources for literature, music, and science.

American Library Association (ALA)—All ages
www.ala.org
Identifies great Web sites for children, including Math Cats (www.mathcats.com), a registered trademark of Wendy A. Petti. This site includes playful open-ended games and explorations of math concepts.

Building Blocks—Foundations for Mathematical Thinking, PreK–Grade 2.
www.gse.buffalo.edu/org/buildingblocks/
Under the guidance of Douglas H. Clements and Julie Sarama, University at Buffalo, State University of New York, this site presents mathematics curriculum materials in line with NCTM standards.

Figure This! Family Corner—PreK–Grade 6
www.figurethis.org/fc/family_corner.htm
This site provides resources to help teachers communicate with parents about math and suggests activities families can do together to explore math.

Math is Everywhere—PreK–K
www.sesamestreet.org/parents/math
This site provides helpful information for teachers and families about how to integrate math into children's daily lives and experiences. The site includes videos, activities, a parent guide, and ideas for teachers.

Math Perspectives—PreK–Grade 6
www.mathperspectives.com
This site provides teachers with tools, strategies, and assessments.

National Association for the Education of Young Children (NAEYC)—PreK–Grade 3
www.naeyc.org
Provides resources to members. You can download the position statement (issued jointly with the National Council of Teachers of Mathematics), entitled *Early Childhood*

Mathematics: Promoting Good Beginnings, at www.naeyc.org/files/naeyc/file/positions/ psmath.pdf.

National Council of Teachers of Mathematics (NCTM)—PreK–Grade 12
http://nctm.org
Provides a large selection of educational materials and resources. The *Curriculum Focal Points for Prekindergarten Through Grade 8 Mathematics: Related Expectations from Principles and Standards,* are available for purchase at www.nctm.org/standards/focalpoints. aspx?id=280.

The Principles and Standards are available at
www.nctm.org/standards/content.aspx?id=4294967312. The standards are supported by both i-math online interactive math investigations and e-math selected electronic examples from the electronic version of the Principles and Standards. There is nothing here for very young children, although some of the examples could be adapted.

National Council of Supervisors of Mathematics (NCSM)—Kindergarten–Grade 12
www.ncsmonline.org
This Web site has a nice section of teaching resources beginning with kindergarten. There are science and math materials and suggestions such as what manipulative to choose to teach what concept. This could be adapted for younger children.

Common Core Standards—Kindergarten–Grade 12
www.ncsmonline.org/docs/resources/ccss/CCSSI_Math%20Standards%20Expanded.pdf
The Common Core standards were recently released and provide comprehensive standards and expectations in mathematics for grade K–12.

Head Start Early Childhood Learning & Knowledge Center (ECLKC)—PreK–K
http://eclkc.ohs.acf.hhs.gov/hslc/ecdh/eecd/Domains%20of%20Child%20Development/ Mathematics
This site provides many resources about mathematics, including activities, teacher guides for using books to explore math concepts, family letters, and webinars on various math concepts.

National Head Start Association—PreK
www.nhsa.org
Good resources in all curriculum areas for members of this organization.

Smithsonian Folkway Recordings—All ages
www.folkways.si.edu
Wonderful educational recordings—tapes and CDs—by Ella Jenkins, Hap Palmer, Rosemary Hallum, and others. There are many that deal with beginning math concepts, such as "Counting Games and Rhythms for the Little Ones" and "Dancing Numerals."

Educational Activities—All ages
www.edact.com
Distributes educational CDs and DVDs.

Carol Hurst's Children's Literature Site—PreK–Grade 3

www.carolhurst.com

A very good Web site for locating excellent children's literature by curriculum area. The books are annotated. Many good fiction and nonfiction math books are listed by topic.

Math Forum at Drexel University—Kindergarten–Grade 12

http://mathforum.org

The forum features math resources by subject. You can also access Dr. Math, Teacher Exchange, and Key Issues in Math Education, among others.

Exemplars—Kindergarten–Grade 12

www.exemplars.com

Offers classroom-tested, standards-based assessment and instruction materials, featuring math tasks and free samples.

Hallum, R., & Glass, H. *Dancing Numerals*

www.edact.com/files/lyrics/CD537.pdf

Introduces counting, geometric shapes, patterns, and simple addition and subtraction concepts with age-appropriate physical movement.

For Families

An increasing number of families have regular access to the Internet. The following Web sites provide valuable information and ideas for families to help children think about math at home. If parents do not have access, consider including some of the recommendations in your regular family newsletters.

U.S. Department of Education, Office of Educational Research and Improvement, National Institute on Early Childhood Development and Education—PreK–Grade 3

www2.ed.gov/pubs/EarlyMath

This site has wonderful ideas for parents to help their children with math concepts in an everyday context. All of the activities are good, and none are threatening. You can download a copy of their excellent math publication for parents and their 2- to 5-year-old children, "Where Learning Begins—Mathematics." Teachers can easily use these ideas as well.

U.S. Department of Education, Office of Communications and Outreach Helping your Child *Learn Mathematics*—PreK–Grade 5

www2.ed.gov/parents/academic/help/math/math.pdf

EQUALS and Family Math—PreK–Grade 3

www.lawrencehallofscience.org/equals/

The EQUALS programs at the Lawrence Hall of Science, University of California at Berkeley, provide workshops and curriculum material in mathematics for teachers, parents, families, and community members. Their book *Family Math for Young Children: Comparing* is an excellent resource for teachers seeking to provide guidance to families about supporting math at home.

For Kids—PreK–Grade 8

The following are Web sites that provide online educational math games for children of all ages.
IXL Learning
www.ixl.com/1b
With membership, teachers and families can track children's progress in skills as they play.

A Maths Dictionary for Kids—Kindergarten–Grade 6
www.amathsdictionaryforkids.com
A math dictionary for K–6 students, with definitions of 500 common terms. There are also interactive math activities grouped by age.

The Rainforest Maths Web site
www.rainforestmaths.com

Learning Planet
www.learningplanet.com
Interactive games for children—including math

Gamequarium
www.gamequarium.com

PBS Kids
http://pbskids.org/dinosaurtrain/games

Index